MasterChef
1996

MasterChef 1996

Foreword by Loyd Grossman

General Editor: Janet Illsley

EBURY PRESS
LONDON

First published 1996

1 3 5 7 9 10 8 6 4 2

Compilation copyright © Union Pictures 1996
Recipes copyright © The Contributors 1996
Foreword © Loyd Grossman 1996
Introduction © Richard Bryan 1996
Back cover photograph © Richard Farley 1996

First published in the United Kingdom in 1996 by Ebury Press,
Random House, 20 Vauxhall Bridge Road, London SW1V 2SA

Random House Australia (Pty) Limited
20 Alfred Street, Milsons Point, Sydney,
New South Wales 2061, Australia

Random House New Zealand Limited
18 Poland Road, Glenfield
Auckland 10, New Zealand

Random House South Africa (Pty) Limited
PO BOX 337, Bergvlei, South Africa

Random House UK Limited Reg. No. 954009

A CIP catalogue record for this book is available from the British Library

ISBN: 0 09 181462 6

MasterChef 1996
A Union Pictures production for BBC North

Series devised by Franc Roddam
Executive Producers: Bradley Adams and Richard Kalms
Producer and Director: Richard Bryan
Associate Producer: Glynis Robertson
Production Co-ordinator: Julia Park

General Editor: Janet Illsley
Design: Clive Dorman

Typeset in Garamond by Clive Dorman & Co.
Printed and bound in Great Britain by Mackays of Chatham plc, Kent.

Papers used by Ebury Press are natural recyclable products made from wood
grown in sustainable forests.

Contents

Cookery Notes

- All recipes serve 4.
- Both metric and imperial measures are given for the recipes. Follow one set of measurements only, not a combination, because they are not interchangeable.
- All spoon measures are level unless otherwise stated.
- Use fresh herbs unless otherwise suggested.
- Ovens must be preheated to the specified temperature. Grills should also be preheated.
- Size 2 eggs should be used except where otherwise specified. Free-range eggs are recommended.
- Stocks should be freshly made if possible. Alternatively buy good quality ready-made stock.

Foreword

An English friend said to me that when something happens once in Britain it's an event; when it happens twice it's an institution. By that definition MasterChef has grown into an almost venerable institution since it was first broadcast in 1990. The reasons for MasterChef's longevity have remained remarkably consistent since our earliest programmes. The fact that we have tried to mix good humour with good cookery; the fascination of hearing some of our top chefs and most prominent actors, politicians, sportsmen and business people share their views and feelings about food; and above all the passion and inventiveness that comes from a truly amateur competition where our contestants are motivated solely by the love of food – a love which they can share with family, friends and viewers.

MasterChef has also become a barometer of our rapidly evolving national taste and MasterChef 1996 was another gastronomic state of the nation. What are our favourite ingredients this year? Scallops, lamb, Aberdeen Angus, sea bass, and berries feature strongly. In truth, these are quite pricey raw materials given a budget of £30 and the requirement to cook a very special three-course meal for four. They indicate an increasing awareness of the importance of carefully selecting top quality materials, and cooking and serving them with great restraint. The classic computer programmers dictum "Rubbish in, rubbish out" applies to food too. The days of using incredibly elaborate techniques to disguise less than perfect ingredients are long gone – today's cooks and eaters want quality to shine through.

It is well worth remembering as you study this year's menus that the priciest ingredients could be happily matched with much more humble and cheaper – though no less delicious – foods too: crab which figures in a few recipes is a good example of a keenly priced yet still luxurious ingredient. And all the judges and I were thrilled by the skill and thoughtfulness that went into so many of this year's most modest dishes – potatoes, pasta and rice all shone brilliantly. As always the British genius for puddings was much in evidence, hardly a week went by which didn't feature three astonishing puddings as you will hear from the judges comments as the series unfolds.

Overall this year also saw an increased awareness of flavour. More fresh herbs than ever before, a continued experimentation with exotic spices and seasonings, and a willingness to tempt the judges with dishes many of us hadn't tasted or even heard of before, marked many of this year's menus. While dishes which owed much to French classical techniques appeared now and again, the Italian presence was stronger than ever, and a number of recipes reflected our love of Asian cuisines.

Once again I'd like to dedicate this book to our contestants, not just for their splendid cooking, but for their good humour and willingness to have a go.

Loyd Grossman

Introduction

Each year this book details the recipes of the twenty-seven contestants who battle it out in the red, yellow and blue kitchens for the British Grand Prix for Amateur Chefs. Whoever has the talent, determination and good fortune to make it to the final, every one of our cooks is already a two-time winner in the process of selection which takes the MasterChef production team almost half the year.

After Loyd Grossman's call for contestants in the previous year's final programme, we receive thousands of requests for an application form and information kit. At this stage some people realise that, as well as being tremendous fun, the competition is likely to be fairly time-consuming: but on the basis of the completed forms received, we select the best sixteen applicants from each of ten or eleven areas of Britain, holding regional 'cook-offs' in catering colleges in their major cities. In true MasterChef tradition, these have a time limit of two-and-a-half hours and three hungry judges, of whom I am delighted to be one, to taste the dishes. My co-judges are a top chef and a senior lecturer from the host college.

After deliberation, cogitation and digestion equal to anything Loyd will experience, we select the three contestants who will represent their region, or combined regions, on television. A few weeks later I visit each of those selected with my camera crew to record the short biography with which we introduce them on the programme, and they are then brought to the studios for the competition itself. I would like to offer my heartfelt thanks to this year's twenty-seven valiant cooks whose lives we have taken over somewhat in the months leading up to the studio contest.

Over the years we have received several requests for the book to be published earlier, so that viewers are able to cook for themselves some of the MasterChef dishes within days, rather than months, of seeing them prepared by the contestants in the red, yellow and blue kitchens. Many of you have also asked for the recipes to be listed by courses so that it is easier to find a specific dish. I hope that you will like the book's new format. All our production team feel that the recipes this year are amongst the best ever, and we hope that, when you come to try them, you and your family and friends will wholeheartedly agree with us.

Richard Bryan

Soups
& Starters

Arbroath Smokie and Mussel Chowder

Arbroath smokies are small smoked haddock, about 10 inches (25 cm) long and pale bronze in colour.

500 g (1¼ lb) fresh mussels in shell
15 ml (1 tbsp) butter
1 leek, white part only, finely chopped
350 ml (12 fl oz) fish stock (see below)
250 g (9 oz) potato, peeled and cubed
generous sprinkling of chopped marjoram or
 oregano
1 medium filleted Arbroath smokie, about
 200 g (7 oz), flaked
few saffron strands
100 g (3½ oz) fresh garden peas
200 ml (7 fl oz) full-cream milk
salt and freshly ground black pepper
150 ml (¼ pint) double cream

1 Scrub the mussels thoroughly in cold water and remove the beards. Discard any open mussels which do not close when tapped firmly.

2 Melt the butter in a saucepan, add the leek, cover and sweat until softened. Add the fish stock, cubed potato and herbs. Bring to the boil, lower the heat and simmer for about 15 minutes until the potatoes are cooked.

3 Put the mussels in a large saucepan with about 120 ml (4 fl oz) water. Cover with a tight-fitting lid and steam over a high heat for about 4 minutes until the mussels are open. Drain and remove most of the mussels from their shells; leave a few whole for garnish. Discard any unopened ones.

4 Add the smoked fish, saffron, peas, mussels and milk to the leek and potato mixture. Stir well and bring to simmering point. Lower the heat and season with pepper to taste, adding salt only if needed. Simmer gently for 4-5 minutes, then add the cream and heat through, but do not allow to boil. Check the seasoning. Ladle into warmed soup bowls and serve at once.

Fish Stock: To make this, use the heads and spines from 6-7 haddock or other white fish. Place in a saucepan with 1 onion, 1 carrot, 1 fennel bulb, a handful of parsley sprigs, a few black peppercorns and a little salt. Add a glass of white wine and 350 ml (12 fl oz) water. Bring to the boil, lower the heat and simmer, uncovered, for 20 minutes. Strain through a fine sieve.

Oxtail Soup with Herb Dumplings

15 ml (1 tbsp) butter
900 g (2 lb) oxtail, in 2.5 cm (1 inch) pieces
2 onions, diced
1 small clove garlic, crushed
1 thyme sprig
1 bay leaf
salt and freshly ground black pepper
½ bottle red wine
900 ml (1½ pints) beef stock
30 ml (2 tbsp) Madeira

Herb Dumplings:
110 g (4 oz) shredded suet
225 g (8 oz) self-raising flour
large pinch of salt
1 egg, beaten
60-90 ml (2-3 fl oz) water
300 ml (½ pint) chicken stock

To Garnish:
chopped parsley

1 Heat half of the butter in a large heavy-based saucepan or flameproof casserole. Add the oxtail and fry, turning, until browned on all sides, then remove from the pan. Add the onions and garlic to the fat remaining in the pan and fry until golden brown.

2 Return the oxtail to the pan and add the herbs, seasoning and half of the red wine. Let bubble until the wine has almost totally reduced. Add the meat stock, cover and simmer very gently over a low heat for 1½ hours.

3 Meanwhile, make the dumplings. Mix the shredded suet, flour and salt together in a bowl. Mix in the egg and sufficient water to form a fairly firm dough. Shape into 2.5 cm (1 inch) balls.

4 Add the Madeira to the soup and simmer for a further 15-30 minutes until the meat starts to fall from the bone.

5 Meanwhile, bring the chicken stock to the boil in a saucepan. Add the dumplings, lower the heat, cover and simmer for approximately 20 minutes until they are light and fluffy.

6 About 5 minutes before the end of cooking, transfer the dumplings from the stock to the soup, using a slotted spoon. Ladle the soup and dumplings into warmed bowls. Garnish with chopped parsley to serve.

Roasted Red Pepper and Tomato Soup

Vegetable Stock:
25 g (1 oz) butter
1 onion, chopped
2 carrots, chopped
450 ml (1½ pints) water
bunch of herbs (eg parsley, thyme and rosemary)
salt and freshly ground black pepper

Soup:
450 g (1 lb) tomatoes
6 red peppers
a little olive oil, for basting
600 ml (1 pint) vegetable stock (see above)

To Finish:
150 ml (¼ pint) single cream (at room temperature)
basil leaves, to garnish

1 To prepare the stock, melt the butter in a saucepan. Add the vegetables and sauté gently until softened. Add the water, herbs and seasoning. Bring to the boil, lower the heat and simmer, covered, for 20-30 minutes. Strain the stock through a fine sieve, discarding the vegetables and herbs.

2 Halve the peppers and remove the core and seeds. Lay cut-side down on a strong baking tray.

3 Immerse the tomatoes in a bowl of boiling water and leave for 1 minute. Remove with a slotted spoon and peel away the skins.

4 Place the tomatoes on the tray with the peppers. Sprinkle with oil and roast in a preheated oven at 200°C (400°F) mark 6 for 45-50 minutes until slightly charred round the edges.

5 Place the peppers in a covered dish for 5-10 minutes; the steam created will help to lift the skins. Peel away the skins from the peppers. Put the tomatoes and peppers in a blender or food processor with the stock. Process until smooth.

6 Return the soup to the saucepan and reheat gently. Adjust the seasoning. Serve in warmed bowls, topped with a generous swirl of cream and a basil leaf.

Chilled Thai Soup

This soup is served accompanied by a Thai Salad and Prawn Won Ton (see opposite).

4 red peppers, halved, cored and seeded
50 g (2 oz) fresh root ginger, peeled and cut into chunks
3 cloves garlic, peeled
1-2 red chillies, halved and seeded (see note)
600 ml (1 pint) chicken stock
300 ml (½ pint) single cream
juice of 1 lime
5 ml (1 tsp) Thai fish sauce (nam pla)
salt
dash of tabasco (optional)
1 bunch coriander sprigs

1 Put the red peppers, ginger, garlic and chillies in a saucepan with the chicken stock. Bring to the boil, then lower the heat and simmer, covered, for 30-40 minutes, until the garlic is softened.

2 Allow the soup to cool slightly, discard the ginger pieces, then transfer to a blender or food processor and work until smooth. Pass through a sieve into a bowl and chill in the refrigerator.

3 Add the cream, lime juice and fish sauce. Check the seasoning, adding a little salt and/or tabasco if necessary.

4 Set aside a few coriander leaves for garnish. Chop the rest finely and add to the soup.

5 Serve garnished with the reserved coriander leaves and accompanied by the Thai Salad with Prawn Won Ton.

Note: Chillies vary in strength, from the long thin kind to the fiery little West Indian 'bonnet' chillies. Aim for a soup which has some 'kick' but is not too fiery.

Thai Salad and Prawn Won Ton

1 small head Chinese leaves
8 spring onions
15-30 ml (1-2 tbsp) sesame oil
4 shallots, finely sliced
4 cloves garlic, finely sliced
15 ml (1 tbsp) light soy sauce
15 ml (1 tbsp) caster sugar
juice of 1 lime
2 red chillies
50 g (2 oz) fresh root ginger

Won Ton:
8 raw Tiger prawns
8 won ton wrappers
oil for deep-frying

1 Shred the Chinese leaves as finely as possible, discarding any flabby green leaves.

2 Trim the spring onions, leaving about 5 cm (2 inches) of the green tops attached. Make vertical cuts in the green part to form a brush, then immerse in a bowl of cold water and leave to open out.

3 For the dressing, heat the sesame oil in a pan, add the shallots and garlic and fry until deep brown in colour. There should be about 15 ml (1 tbsp) oil left in the pan; if necessary add a little more. Add the soy sauce and sugar to the pan and stir until the sugar has dissolved.

4 Transfer the dressing to a bowl or jug and add the lime juice to taste; aim for a balance of sweet and sour flavours.

5 Halve and deseed the chillies and shred very finely. Peel the ginger root and slice thinly into small, round 'chips'. Set aside.

6 To prepare the won ton, peel the prawns and, using a sharp knife, remove the black vein from the back of each one. Put some of the salad dressing into a small bowl. Dip each prawn into this dressing, then wrap in a won ton wrapper, pinching it either side of the prawn to seal and form a cracker shape.

7 Heat the oil in a deep-fat fryer until a piece of bread dropped in will turn golden and crisp in about 1 minute. Add the chillies and fry for a few seconds; drain on kitchen paper. Fry the ginger until golden; drain on kitchen paper. Add the won ton to the oil and deep-fry for 3-4 minutes until golden brown, drain on kitchen paper.

8 To serve, pile the shredded Chinese leaves on each serving plate. Drizzle over the dressing, spooning some of the garlic and shallots on top. Scatter over the deep-fried chilli and ginger. Top with the spring onion 'brushes' and won ton. Serve at once.

Crab Salad with Chilli and Herb Dressing

Dressing:
5 ml (1 tsp) coriander seeds
2 star anise
4 lemon grass stalks
2 green chillis, halved and seeded
2 cloves garlic, peeled
5 cm (2 inch) piece fresh root ginger, peeled
juice of 2 limes
juice of 1 lemon (approximately)
90 ml (6 tbsp) water
90 ml (6 tbsp) olive oil
30 ml (2 tbsp) sunflower oil
90 ml (6 tbsp) Thai fish sauce
  (approximately)
pinch of sugar

Crab Salad:
½ cucumber
1 large or 2 small dressed crabs (white meat only)
salt and freshly ground black pepper
60 ml (4 tbsp) chopped fresh coriander

To Serve:
French country-style bread

1 To make the dressing, lightly crush the coriander seeds and star anise. Roughly chop the lemon grass, chillis, garlic and ginger and place in a bowl with the coriander seeds and star anise. Add the lime juice, lemon juice, water, olive oil, sunflower oil, fish sauce and sugar. Whisk together until evenly blended, then set aside to infuse for at least 30 minutes. Strain the dressing through a fine sieve, discarding the chopped flavourings. Taste and adjust the flavouring, adding a little more fish sauce or lemon juice as required.

2 Peel the cucumber, halve lengthwise and scoop out the seeds. Cut the flesh into julienne strips. Sprinkle with a little salt and leave to drain in a colander for 15 minutes. Rinse thoroughly under cold running water and pat dry with kitchen paper.

3 Season the white crab meat with salt and pepper to taste.

4 Pile the crab meat in the centre of each serving plate. Surround with the cucumber julienne. Whisk the dressing, then drizzle a little over the crab meat and pool the rest around it. Sprinkle with chopped coriander. Serve with French country-style bread to mop up the dressing.

King Prawns with Pear

200 g (7 oz) raw King prawns
50 ml (2 fl oz) chilli oil
shredded zest and juice of 1 lime
30 g (1¼ oz) creamed coconut
2 cloves garlic, crushed
10 g (⅓ oz) finely grated fresh root ginger
4 pears (preferably Conference)
salt and freshly ground black pepper
10 g (⅓ oz) roughly chopped coriander

To Serve:
oak leaf lettuce leaves

1 Plunge the prawns into a large pan of boiling water and cook for 30 seconds or until they just change colour. Remove and cool under running cold water. Shell the prawns, leaving the tail shell in tact. De-vein and pat dry with kitchen paper.

2 For the marinade, mix half the chilli oil with the lime zest and juice, creamed coconut, garlic and ginger in a shallow dish. Add the prawns and turn gently to ensure they are well coated with the mixture. Leave to marinade in a cool place for 1½-2 hours.

3 Peel and core the pears and cut each one into about 6 large chunks. Arrange a bed of lettuce leaves on each serving plate.

4 Heat the remaining chilli oil in a wok until very hot. Add the prawns together with the marinade and quickly stir-fry for 1 minute. Add the pear chunks and fry for a further 1 minute. Season with salt and pepper to taste and add the coriander.

5 To serve, divide the prawns and pear chunks between the lettuce-lined serving plates and dress with the cooking juices from the wok. Serve immediately.

Smoked Bacon and Queenie Salad with a Warm Vinaigrette

sufficient mixed salad leaves for 4 (eg rocket, lamb's lettuce, radicchio)
4 rashers smoked streaky bacon, derinded
350 g (12 oz) cleaned queen scallops
15 ml (1 tbsp) groundnut oil

Dressing:
50 ml (3½ tbsp) groundnut oil
15 ml (1 tbsp) red wine vinegar
5 ml (1 tsp) balsamic vinegar
salt and freshly ground black pepper

1 Arrange a small pile of salad leaves in the middle of each serving plate.

2 Fry the bacon in its own fat in a heavy-based frying pan until cooked and almost crisped. Remove the rashers from the pan and cut into small pieces, reserving the bacon fat in the frying pan.

3 Put all of the ingredients for the dressing in a small saucepan and heat through, but do not boil.

4 Meanwhile, add the 15 ml (1 tbsp) oil to the bacon fat in the frying pan and heat. Season the scallops lightly with salt, drop into the frying pan and fry quickly for 45 seconds to 1 minute on each side, depending on size; do not overcook or they will become rubbery.

5 Toss the queenies with the warm dressing, ensuring they are evenly coated, then add the bacon and toss well.

6 Divide the scallop and bacon mixture between the serving plates, spooning it on top of the salad leaves. Drizzle over any remaining dressing and serve at once.

Mussels with Blue Vinney Sauce

1.8 kg (4 lb) mussels in shells
125 g (4 oz) blue Vinney cheese, crumbled
125 ml (4 fl oz) single cream
25 g (1 oz) unsalted butter
*2 leeks (white and pale green part only),
  finely chopped*
600 ml (1 pint) dry cider
60 ml (4 tbsp) finely chopped parsley

To Serve:
Walnut Bread (see right)

1 Scrub the mussels thoroughly under cold running water, scraping off any barnacles with a sharp knife, and pulling off the 'beards' protruding from the shells. Discard any mussels with cracked shells and any which remain open when sharply tapped with the back of a knife. Set aside in a colander.

2 Put the cheese and cream in a food processor or blender and process or mash together until the cheese is well broken up.

3 Melt the butter in a large pan, add the leeks and cook gently until soft. Add the cider and bring to the boil. Tip in the mussels and cook for 3-5 minutes until the shells are open; discard any that remain closed.

4 Pour the cream and cheese mixture into the pan and stir until well amalgamated and heated through.

5 Tip the mussels and sauce into warmed large soup plates and sprinkle with the chopped parsley. Serve at once, accompanied by the Walnut Bread (see right).

Walnut Bread

This is a close-textured bread, which keeps well.

300 g (10 oz) strong plain wholemeal flour
175 g (6 oz) rye flour
5 ml (1 tsp) salt
*7 g (¼ oz) fresh yeast, or 5 ml (1 tsp) dried
  yeast*
150-300 ml (¼-½ pint) warm water
50 g (2 oz) walnuts, chopped
10 ml (2 tsp) caraway seeds
15 ml (1 tbsp) walnut oil

1 Sift the flours and salt together into a mixing bowl. (If the flour is very cold put the bowl in a warm place for a few minutes.)

2 Cream the yeast with a little of the warm water in a small bowl and leave for 5 minutes in a warm place or until frothy on the surface.

3 Add the walnuts, caraway seeds and walnut oil to the flour. Now add the creamed yeast and incorporate enough warm water to make a stiff dough. Knead the dough for 5 minutes.

4 Put the dough in a bowl, cover with oiled cling film and leave in a warm place for 1½ hours; it will only rise very slightly.

5 Knead the dough again lightly, then shape into a loaf and place in a greased 900 g (2 lb) loaf tin. Leave in a warm place to prove for a further 1 hour.

6 Bake the loaf in a preheated oven at 220°C (425°F) mark 7 for approximately 45 minutes, until the loaf will turn out of the tin easily and sounds hollow when tapped on the bottom. Transfer to a wire rack. Cut into thin slices to serve.

Seared Scallop and Pancetta Salad with an Orange Saffron Dressing

*100 g (3½ oz) pancetta, derinded and cut
    into strips
a little olive oil, for cooking
3 bunches watercress, stalks removed
12 medium-large scallops, cleaned and
    halved
sea salt and freshly ground black pepper*

Orange Saffron Dressing:
*pinch of saffron threads
20 ml (4 tsp) olive oil
2.5 ml (½ tsp) sherry vinegar
15 ml (1 tbsp) orange juice
15 ml (1 tbsp) finely chopped orange zest
½ clove garlic, finely chopped
pinch of cayenne pepper
pinch of caster sugar*

1 For the dressing, infuse the saffron threads in 5 ml (1 tsp) hot water for 15 minutes. In a bowl, whisk together the oil, vinegar and orange juice, then mix in the saffron and all the other ingredients, seasoning with salt and pepper to taste. Place in a screw-topped jar and leave to stand for at least 30 minutes.

2 Meanwhile, gently fry the pancetta in a little oil until crisp. Divide the watercress between 4 individual serving plates.

3 Preheat a skillet or heavy-based frying pan. Brush the scallops with olive oil and season with salt and pepper. Add to the hot pan and cook over a moderately high heat for 1 minute each side.

4 Arrange the scallops on top of the watercress, and sprinkle over the crisp pancetta. Shake the dressing to emulsify, then pour over the salad. Serve immediately.

Nage of Scallops with a Vegetable Julienne

*1 carrot, peeled
50 g (2 oz) celeriac, peeled
1 small leek, trimmed
20 g (¾ oz) unsalted butter
500 ml (16 fl oz) fish stock
salt and freshly ground black pepper
100 ml (3½ fl oz) whipping cream
2.5 ml (½ tsp) ground ginger
6 king scallops, cleaned
chopped chives, to garnish*

1 Cut the vegetables into fine julienne. Melt the butter in a sauté pan, add the vegetables and sweat for 2 minutes. Add the fish stock, bring to the boil and simmer for about 3 minutes. Check the seasoning.

2 Meanwhile, remove the corals from the scallops, then cut each white scallop in half horizontally.

3 Drain the vegetables and keep warm. Return the stock to the pan, add the cream, ginger and scallops and cook for 2 minutes. Check the seasoning.

4 To serve, place a mound of vegetable julienne in the centre of each warmed soup plate. Distribute 3 scallop pieces around the vegetables and pour a generous amount of sauce over the scallops, avoiding covering the vegetables. Scatter chopped chives on top and serve immediately.

Salad of Queen Scallops and Crispy Smoked Bacon with Walnut and Sesame Oil Dressing

125 g (4 oz) lean smoked bacon
125 g (4 oz) salad leaves (eg baby spinach, frisée, oak leaf lettuce)
175 g (6 oz) queen scallops, cleaned
knob of butter
10 ml (2 tsp) light olive oil

Dressing:
15 ml (1 tbsp) walnut oil
15 ml (1 tbsp) sesame oil
45 ml (1 tbsp) light olive oil
30 ml (2 tbsp) sherry vinegar
15 ml (1 tbsp) finely chopped parsley
salt and freshly ground black pepper

1 Cut each bacon rasher into 3 or 4 lengths and twist around a chopstick to form coils. Remove the bacon twists from the chopstick and place on a grill rack. Cook under a preheated grill, turning occasionally, until crisp; keep warm.

2 Meanwhile, tear the salad leaves into bite-sized pieces and place in a large bowl. Put the ingredients for the dressing in a screw-topped jar and shake vigorously until well blended. Pour the dressing over the salad leaves and toss until lightly coated. Arrange a bed of salad leaves on each serving plate.

3 Heat the butter and oil in a heavy-based frying pan, add the scallops and cook over a moderate heat for 2-3 minutes until just tender.

4 Arrange the scallops and bacon twists on the salad leaves and serve at once, while the scallops are still warm.

Sautéed Scallops on a Cream Wine Sauce flavoured with Saffron

12 large scallops, cleaned
salt and freshly ground black pepper
50 g (2 oz) unsalted butter, chilled
1 shallot, finely chopped
6-8 saffron strands
175 ml (6 fl oz) dry white wine
300 ml (½ pint) fish stock
300 ml ½ pint) double cream

To Garnish:
dill sprigs

1 Pat the scallops dry and season with salt and a little pepper; set aside.

2 Melt 15 g (½ oz) of the butter in a saucepan, add the shallot and cook gently until soft.

3 Meanwhile, infuse the saffron strands in 30 ml (2 tbsp) of the wine. Add the rest of the wine to the shallots and reduce to about 30 ml (2 tbsp). Add the stock and reduce over a medium heat until only about 60 ml (2 fl oz) liquid remains.

4 Strain into a clean pan and stir in the cream. Simmer over a medium heat, whisking continuously, until the sauce is thick enough to lightly coat the back of a spoon. Add the saffron-infused wine and reduce a little more. Whisk in 25 g (1 oz) butter, a small piece at a time; keep warm.

5 To cook the scallops, melt the remaining 15 g (½ oz) butter in a sauté pan. Add the scallops and cook over a medium heat for 1 minute on each side.

6 Place 3 scallops on each warmed serving plate and surround with the sauce. Garnish with dill sprigs and serve immediately.

Seared Scallops with Spring Greens and Red Pepper Sauce

12 medium scallops, cleaned
salt and freshly ground black pepper
15 ml (1 tbsp) olive oil

Red Pepper Sauce:
15 ml (1 tbsp) olive oil
1 celery stick, finely chopped
1 shallot, finely chopped
2 medium red peppers, cored, seeded and
    finely chopped
1 clove garlic, finely chopped
small bunch of parsley, stalks only (flat-leaf
    if possible)
600 ml (1 pint) fish stock
1 glass dry white wine
100 ml (3½ fl oz) double cream
salt and freshly ground white pepper

Spring Greens:
15 ml (1 tbsp) olive oil
1 small clove garlic, finely chopped
400 g (14 oz) spring greens, shredded
squeeze of lemon juice, to taste

1 First make the sauce. Heat the olive oil in a heavy-based saucepan and add the vegetables, garlic and parsley stalks. Add the fish stock and wine and bring to the boil. Lower the heat and simmer for 15 minutes until the vegetables are tender. Transfer the mixture to a blender or food processor and work to a purée. Pass through a sieve and return to the clean pan. Bring to the boil and reduce by two thirds, then adjust the seasoning. Stir in the cream, reheat and keep warm.

2 Prepare the spring greens. Heat the olive oil in a large pan, add the garlic and fry for a few seconds, then add the spring greens with just the water clinging to the leaves after washing. Cover and cook for 3-4 minutes until wilted. Season with salt and pepper, and add lemon juice to taste; keep warm.

3 Put the scallops in a bowl and season with salt and pepper. Add the 15 ml (1 tbsp) olive oil and toss to coat the scallops lightly with oil. Heat a heavy-based non-stick frying pan or griddle over a high heat until smoking. Add the scallops in one layer and sear for 30-45 seconds on each side, depending on size. Place a mound of greens in the centre of each warmed serving plate. Arrange the scallops on top and pour the red pepper sauce around. Serve immediately.

Seafood Pastry Chests with Red Pepper Sauce

250 g (9 oz) ready-made puff pastry
beaten egg, mixed with a little milk, to glaze

Sauce:
10 ml (2 tsp) butter
25 g (1 oz) shallots, chopped
100 g (4 oz) red pepper, skinned, seeded and
  chopped
100 g (4 oz) tomatoes, skinned, seeded and
  chopped
40 ml (3 tbsp) double cream
salt and freshly ground black pepper

Filling:
10 ml (2 tsp) butter
3-4 shallots, finely chopped
30 ml (2 tbsp) chopped parsley
1 clove garlic, chopped
100 ml (3½ fl oz) fish stock
50 ml (2 fl oz) dry white wine
60 g (2 oz) salmon fillet, skinned
60 g (2 oz) cleaned squid pouches, cut into
  rings
60 g (2 oz) small cleaned scallops
50 ml (2 fl oz) double cream
pinch of cayenne pepper
salt and freshly ground black pepper
8 asparagus tips
60 g (2 oz) cooked peeled prawns

To Garnish:
dill sprigs

1 Roll out the pastry on a lightly floured surface to a rectangle, approximately 5 mm (¼ inch) thick. Trim the edges and cut 4 rectangles, measuring about 6 x 10 cm (2½ x 4 inches). Round off the corners.

2 Leaving a 5 mm (¼ inch) margin around the edge, score a cross-cross on each rectangle, cutting about halfway through the depth. Finally, cut around the margin, to the same depth; make sure you do not cut all the way through. Chill in the refrigerator for at least 30 minutes before baking.

3 Meanwhile, make the sauce. Melt the butter in a pan, add the chopped shallots and sweat gently until soft. Add the chopped red pepper and cook for 4 minutes, then add the tomatoes and cook for a further 3 minutes. Stir in the cream and season with salt and pepper to taste. Transfer to a blender or food processor and work until smooth, then pass through a sieve into a clean pan.

4 Brush the pastry with the beaten egg wash. Bake in a preheated oven at 190°C (375°F) mark 5 for about 10 minutes until golden brown. Carefully cut around the rim and lift off the lids; set aside. Remove the loose inner pastry to create more space for the filling.

5 For the filling, melt the butter in a pan, add the chopped shallots, parsley and garlic, and sweat over a low heat for a few minutes. Increase the heat and add the fish stock and white wine. Bring to a simmer, then add the salmon fillets, together with the squid and scallops. Poach gently until the salmon is firm to touch, then remove with a slotted spoon and flake into a warm bowl. Poach the squid and scallops for a further 10 minutes, then remove with a slotted spoon; add to the flaked fish.

6 Increase the heat and reduce the cooking liquid by a third, then add the cream, cayenne pepper and salt and pepper to taste.

7 Meanwhile, cook the asparagus in lightly salted boiling water until tender but still crisp; refresh and drain thoroughly.

8 Carefully fold the prawns, salmon, squid and scallops into the reduced cooking liquid. Heat through gently, then spoon the filling into the pastry cases.

9 To serve, gently reheat the sauce and pool on warmed serving plates. Position a seafood pastry chest in the centre. Pop the asparagus tips into the pastry chests and replace the lids, setting them slightly off centre. Garnish with dill and serve at once.

Seafood Dumplings

50 g (2 oz) chicken breast fillet
60 g (2 oz) Japanese fish cake
1 salad onion, trimmed
120 g (4 oz) peeled prawns
160 g (5½ oz) canned white crabmeat
15 ml (1 tbsp) cornflour
salt and freshly ground black pepper
30 ready-made dumpling skins

Dipping Sauce:
25 ml (5 tsp) soy sauce
2.5 ml (½ tsp) wasabi (Japanese horseradish),
  or English mustard to taste

To Garnish:
basil leaves

1 Roughly chop the chicken, fish cake and salad onion into pieces and put into a food processor along with the prawns and crabmeat. Process until finely minced.

2 Turn into a bowl and add the cornflour, salt and pepper to taste. Mix well, using your hand, until smooth and evenly blended.

3 Finely shred 18 of the dumpling skins and set aside.

4 Lay the 12 whole dumpling skins on a clean surface and divide the seafood filling between them, positioning it in the centre of each one. Wrap the skin around the filling (at this stage, you don't need to cover the top).

5 Sprinkle the shredded skins over the dumplings to cover the tops.

6 Bring the water to the boil in a steamer. Stand the dumplings on a lightly greased heatproof plate in the steamer. Cover with a thin tea-towel and place the lid on the steamer. Cook over a moderate heat for about 10 minutes.

7 For the dipping sauce, mix together the soy sauce and wasabi or mustard to taste. Divide between 4 tiny serving dishes.

8 Place 3 dumplings on each plate and garnish with the basil leaves. Serve with the dipping sauce.

Note: Ready-made dumpling skins, fish cake and wasabi are obtainable from Japanese and Chinese specialist food stores.

Lobster and Isle of Skye Scampi Risotto

15 ml (1 tbsp) olive oil
125 g (4 oz) butter
2 onions, finely chopped
225 g (8 oz) Arborio (risotto) rice
salt and freshly ground black pepper
1 glass white wine
few saffron strands
900 ml (1½ pints) fish stock
1 cooked shelled lobster, in chunks
6 cooked crayfish, in pieces
juice of 1 lemon
½ glass brandy
50 g (2 oz) Parmesan cheese, freshly grated

To Garnish:
Parmesan shavings

1 Heat the olive oil and 50 g (2 oz) butter in a medium saucepan. Add the onions and fry gently for a few minutes until beginning to soften. Add the rice and stir to coat with the butter. Cook for a few minutes, then season with salt and pepper.

2 Add the wine and cook until it is absorbed, then add the saffron. Gradually add the stock, a ladleful at a time, ensuring each addition is absorbed before adding the next. This process should take about 20 minutes, by which time the rice will be cooked.

3 Melt the remaining butter in a sauté pan, add the lobster and crayfish meat and sauté for a few minutes to heat through. Season with salt and pepper and add a squeeze of lemon juice to taste. Add the brandy and cook for about 1 minute.

4 Add the Parmesan to the rice and fork through. Pile the rice onto warmed serving plates and top with the lobster and crayfish. Serve topped with Parmesan.

Warm Hot-smoked Teifi Salmon on a bed of Pickled Samphire

1 whole side of smoked salmon, about 700 g (1½ lb)
5 ml (1 tbsp) oak barbecue chips
450 g (1 lb) jar pickled samphire, drained

To Garnish:
salad leaves (eg mache, frisée, chicory)
cucumber slices
virgin olive oil, flavoured with dill, for drizzling

1 Cut vertically through the middle section of the smoked salmon to give four chunky 75 g (3 oz) portions. (Use the rest of the salmon for another occasion.)

2 Soak the oak barbecue chips in water to cover for 20 minutes, then drain and scatter over the base of a wok. Place the salmon on a rack in the wok over the barbecue chips and cover with a domed close-fitting lid. Place over a high heat for 2-3 minutes until smoke starts to emit, then remove the wok from the heat, but do not lift the lid. Leave the salmon to cook in the residual heat for 10-15 minutes.

3 To serve, remove the skin from the warm salmon and place on a bed of pickled samphire on individual plates. Garnish with salad leaves and cucumber slices, drizzled with dill-flavoured olive oil. Serve at once.

Note: Jars of pickled samphire are obtainable from delicatessens, or better still, prepare your own by pickling freshly gathered or purchased samphire in vinegar.

To prepare the flavoured oil, simply steep a handful of dill sprigs in a bottle of virgin olive oil and leave to stand for a few days to allow the flavours to infuse.

Pan-fried Scottish Salmon on Wilted Greens with Spicy Tomato Sauce

4 pieces of salmon fillet, each about 75 g (3 oz), skinned
30 ml (2 tbsp) olive oil
salt and freshly ground black pepper

Sauce:
60 ml (4 tbsp) olive oil
3 shallots, finely chopped
3 cloves garlic, finely chopped
60 ml (4 tbsp) tomato ketchup
75 ml (5 tbsp) pepper-flavoured olive oil
15 ml (1 tbsp) chopped basil

Wilted Greens:
10 ml (2 tsp) basil-flavoured olive oil
sufficient mixed salad leaves for 4 (eg rocket, oak leaf, lamb's lettuce)

To Garnish:
20 ml (4 tsp) basil-flavoured olive oil
basil leaves

1 Brush the salmon fillets with a little of the olive oil. Heat the rest of the oil in a heavy-based frying pan, add the salmon pieces and sauté over a moderate heat for 30 seconds. Turn the fillets over and cook for a further 10 seconds. Transfer to an ovenproof dish and place in a preheated oven at 190°C (375°F) mark 5 for 4-5 minutes. Remove the fish from the oven, season, re-cover and keep warm.

2 Meanwhile, make the sauce. Heat the olive oil in a pan, add the shallots and garlic, and sauté until soft, but not coloured. Stir in the tomato ketchup and cook for 1 minute. Stir in the pepper-flavoured olive oil. Season with salt and pepper to taste and add the chopped basil. Set aside.

3 For the wilted greens, warm 10 ml (2 tsp) basil-flavoured oil in a saucepan. Add the salad leaves and toss gently until they are just wilted. Season with salt and pepper to taste.

4 To serve, put a mound of wilted salad leaves in the centre of each serving plate and top with a piece of salmon. Spoon the sauce around the salad leaves and dot basil oil around the edge of the plate. Garnish with basil leaves and serve immediately.

Note: Excellent flavoured oils are available from delicatessens; alternatively prepare your own by steeping basil sprigs and red peppers in separate bottles of olive oil for a few days.

Salmon and Matzomeal Fish Cakes with an Orange Pepper Sauce

225 g (8 oz) salmon fillet (preferably wild
 salmon)
50 g (2 oz) medium matzomeal
squeeze of lemon juice
1 egg (size 2)
7 g (¼ oz) anchovy paste
15 ml (1 tbsp) chopped dill, or to taste
60 ml (2 fl oz) white wine (approximately)
salt and freshly ground black pepper
4 leeks, cleaned
25 g (1 oz) butter
olive oil, for shallow-frying
1 clove garlic, crushed
15 ml (1 tbsp) sesame oil

Orange Pepper Sauce:
1 orange pepper
3 oz (75 g) Greek yogurt
salt

To Garnish:
dill sprigs
salmon eggs

1 Half-fill a large heavy-based frying pan with water and bring to a simmer. Add the salmon (ensuring there is sufficient water to just cover it) and poach for 12 minutes, until just cooked through. Carefully transfer the salmon to a plate to cool; reserve the cooking liquid. Remove the skin and any residual bones from the salmon, then flake the flesh into a bowl.

2 Add 40 g (1½ oz) of the matzomeal to the salmon. Mix together using a fork, then add the lemon juice, egg, anchovy paste and dill to taste. Stir well, then add the wine, a little at a time, mixing to a smooth paste. Season with salt and pepper to taste. (At this stage, the mixture should look firm but moist, and be a little too soft to shape into cakes. The softer at the stage, the fluffier the eventual fish cakes.) Chill in the refrigerator for at least 30 minutes, to allow the mixture to swell and firm as the matzomeal absorbs the liquid.

3 To make the orange pepper sauce, roast the pepper in a preheated oven at 200°C (400°F) mark 6 for 25 minutes or until the skin is blistered all over. Place in a bowl, cover and allow to cool. Peel away the skin from the pepper, then, halve and remove the seeds. Put the pepper halves in a blender or food processor with the yogurt and work until smooth. Add salt to taste. Set aside.

4 Meanwhile, cut the leeks into 5 cm (2 inch) lengths and blanch in boiling water until barely tender; drain thoroughly. Cut into thin strips and set aside.

5 Heat the reserved salmon poaching liquid in the frying pan until almost but not quite simmering; keep on a very low heat. Form the salmon and matzomeal mix into 12 patties and carefully place in the stock (which should just cover them). Poach for 10 minutes, then lift out the fish cakes with a slotted spoon, drain and dry on kitchen paper. Coat both sides of the fish cakes with matzomeal.

6 Heat half the butter with enough olive oil for shallow frying in the clean, dry frying pan. When hot, lower the heat. Add the garlic to flavour the oil, then remove with a slotted spoon. Add the fish cakes and fry on each side until lightly browned.

7 At the same time, heat the remaining butter and sesame oil in another pan, add the leeks and stir-fry until tender. Warm the sauce in a small pan; do not boil. Drain the fish cakes and leeks on kitchen paper.

8 To serve, pile the leeks in the centre of each warmed serving plate and arrange the fish cakes on top. Surround with pools of orange pepper sauce. Garnish with dill sprigs and salmon eggs, and serve at once.

Salmon and Dill Paupiettes with a Preserved Lemon Relish

Salmon and Dill Paupiettes:
200 g (7 oz) salmon fillet, skinned
1 egg white
100 ml (3½ oz) double cream
large bunch of dill sprigs, stalks removed, finely chopped
salt and freshly ground white pepper
4 slices smoked salmon, about 15 cm (6 inches) square

Lemon Relish:
4 shallots, finely sliced
60 ml (4 tbsp) white wine vinegar
60 ml (4 tbsp) water
12 green beans, cut into 2 cm (¾ inch) lengths
rind of 1 preserved lemon, finely sliced
10-15 ml (2-3 tsp) caster sugar, to taste
salt and freshly ground black pepper

To Garnish:
dill sprigs

1 Put the salmon fillet in a food processor and work until smooth, then press through a sieve into a large bowl. Mix in the egg white, using a wooden spoon. Slowly mix in the cream, a spoonful at a time. Add the chopped dill and season with salt and pepper to taste. Cover and refrigerate for 20 minutes.

2 Meanwhile, make the lemon relish. Put the shallots, wine vinegar and water in a small pan and simmer for about 10 minutes until the liquid is reduced to 30 ml (2 tbsp). Cook the green beans in a large pan of boiling salted water for 2 minutes; drain and refresh in cold water. Add the beans to the vinegar mixture with the preserved lemon rind and sugar. Cook for a further 3 minutes, or until the mixture is the consistency of a relish. Check the seasoning.

3 Half-fill a large shallow pan with water and bring to the boil. Reduce the heat until the water is just below simmering.

4 Lay each smoked salmon slice on a sheet of greaseproof paper and divide the cooled salmon mousseline between the slices. Spread evenly, leaving a margin at the edges. Roll up the salmon paupiettes and wrap tightly in the greaseproof paper, twisting the ends to seal. Carefully lower the paupiettes into the water and poach for approximately 6 minutes or until firm to the touch. Remove, unwrap and cut into 1 cm (¾ inch) slices. Put a spoonful of the lemon relish on each serving plate and surround with the paupiette slices. Garnish with dill sprigs and serve at once.

Grilled Haddock Fillet with a Cheese and Dill Topping

280 g (10 oz) haddock fillet, skinned

Cheese and Dill Topping:
100 g (3½ oz) Philadelphia cream cheese
5 ml (1 tsp) lemon juice
large bunch of dill, chopped
5 ml (1 tsp) caster sugar
salt and freshly ground white pepper

Cranberry and Red Pepper Marmalade:
100 g (3½ oz) fresh or frozen cranberries
1 small red pepper, cored, seeded and finely sliced
15 ml (1 tbsp) olive oil
40 g (1½ oz) caster sugar (approximately)
5 ml (1 tsp) lemon juice
few drops of Thai fish sauce, or to taste

To Garnish:
dill sprigs

1 For the topping, put the cream cheese in a bowl and mix in the lemon juice, dill, sugar and seasoning to taste, until evenly blended.

2 Cut the haddock into four even-sized pieces and cover with the cheese mixture. Place on a baking sheet in the refrigerator for approximately 10 minutes until the cheese mixture is firm.

3 Meanwhile, make the cranberry and red pepper marmalade. Put the cranberries into a heavy-based saucepan. Cover and place over a low heat until the cranberries begin to pop, then remove the lid. Add the sliced red pepper and olive oil. Cook for 2 minutes, stirring occasionally, then add the sugar, lemon juice and fish sauce. Cook for 5 minutes, adding a little water if the mixture is too dry; it should be the consistency of a chutney. Add a little more sugar to taste if the marmalade is too sharp. Allow to cool slightly.

4 Preheat the grill to high. Place the fish on the grill rack and cook under the grill for 2-3 minutes without turning, or until it is cooked through. Transfer to warmed serving plates and put a spoonful of the warm marmalade to one side. Garnish with dill and serve immediately.

Pesto Fish Cakes with a Roasted Red Pepper Salsa

Pesto Fish Cakes:
225 g (8 oz) potatoes
salt and freshly ground black pepper
milk and water, for poaching
1 cod fillet, about 225 g (8 oz), skinned
25 g (1 oz) basil leaves
1 small clove garlic, peeled
7.5 ml (1½ tsp) pine nuts
45 ml (3 tbsp) extra-virgin olive oil
50 g (2 oz) Parmesan cheese, freshly grated
½ egg (size 2), beaten (approximately)
45 ml (3 tbsp) instant (quick-cook) polenta

Roasted Red Pepper Salsa:
4 red peppers, halved, cored and seeded
45 ml (3 tbsp) extra-virgin olive oil
15-30 ml (1-2 tbsp) balsamic vinegar

To Garnish:
Parmesan shavings
basil sprigs

1 For the salsa, place the red peppers, skin-side up, in a shallow baking tin and drizzle over the oil. Roast in a preheated oven at 180°C (350°F) mark 4 for 40 minutes or until the skins are wrinkled and just beginning to blacken at the edges; do not allow to become too charred or the salsa

will be ruined. Transfer the peppers and cooking juices to a bowl and cover the bowl tightly with cling film. Set aside for 1 hour.

2 Peel the potatoes and cook in boiling salted water until soft. Drain thoroughly and mash until smooth.

3 Half-fill a frying pan with a mixture of milk and water. Add the cod fillet (ensuring there is sufficient liquid to just cover it) and poach for about 12 minutes, until the fish starts to flake. Transfer to a plate.

4 To make the pesto, place the basil, garlic, pine nuts and olive oil in a food processor and process to a paste. Transfer to a bowl, stir in the grated Parmesan and set aside.

5 Flake the cod into a bowl and add the mashed potato; there should be roughly equal amounts of fish and potato. Add the pesto and mix thoroughly. Season with salt and pepper to taste. Add approximately half of the beaten egg to bind the mixture. Set aside and leave to cool.

6 When cooled, roll the fish cake mixture into small balls the size of golf balls; flatten slightly. Spread the polenta on a plate and roll the fish cakes in the polenta grains to coat. Place on a grill rack and chill in the refrigerator for 30 minutes before cooking.

7 To make the salsa, skin the roasted peppers, then place in a food processor or blender with the reserved juices and balsamic vinegar. Whizz until smooth, then season with salt and pepper and transfer to a serving bowl.

8 Cook the fish cakes under a preheated hot grill, for about 5 minutes, turning from time to time until golden all over. Transfer to warmed serving plates. Garnish with Parmesan shavings and basil sprigs, and serve at once, accompanied by the red pepper salsa.

Pan-fried Red Mullet with Braised Fennel

140 ml (4½ fl oz) olive oil
4 small fennel bulbs, fronds intact
1 clove garlic, peeled and quartered
salt and freshly ground black pepper
juice of ½ orange
juice of ½ lemon
finely pared zest of 1 orange, in strips
8 red mullet fillets
plain flour, for coating
few drops of balsamic vinegar

1 Heat 45 ml (3 tbsp) olive oil in a heavy-based saucepan. Quarter the fennel bulbs, (setting aside the fronds for the dressing). Add to the hot oil and fry, turning, until beginning to brown. Add the garlic and continue to fry until both fennel and garlic are browned. Add just enough water to come two-thirds of the way up the fennel. Season with salt and pepper. Bring to the boil and simmer, uncovered, until tender.

2 Meanwhile, prepare the dressing. Place 50 ml (2 fl oz) olive oil in a blender or food processor with the orange juice, lemon juice and fennel fronds. Blend until evenly amalgamated. Season to taste, and add a little more oil or lemon juice if necessary to achieve the correct balance. Mix in the orange zest.

3 Heat the remaining 45 ml (3 tbsp) olive oil in a large frying pan over a medium heat. Dust the fish fillets with seasoned flour, add to the pan, skin-side down, and fry for 3-4 minutes until crisp underneath. Turn the fillets over and fry for a further 1 minute.

4 Place the red mullet fillets on warmed serving plates with the fennel. Pour over the dressing and drizzle a little balsamic vinegar into the dressing.

Fillet of Sole wrapped in Spinach with Saffron Rice

8 sole fillets, each about 75 g (3 oz)
250 g (9 oz) spinach, stalks removed
60 g (2½ oz) butter
1 onion, finely diced
100 g (3½ oz) rice
salt and freshly ground black pepper
pinch of saffron strands
5 ml (1 tsp) coriander seeds
2 shallots, finely diced
10-15 ml (2-3 tsp) roughly chopped parsley
2 tomatoes, skinned, seeded and diced
30 ml (2 tbsp) fish stock

1 Rinse the sole fillets and pat dry thoroughly. Roll up each fillet to make paupiettes. Wash the spinach thoroughly in several changes of water, drain and dry well.

2 Heat 40 g (1½ oz) of the butter in a saucepan, add the diced onion and sauté gently until softened but not coloured. Add the rice and cook, stirring, until just transparent. Season with salt and add the saffron. Stir well and add 300 ml (½ pint) water. Cook gently until almost all of the water is absorbed and the rice is fluffy. Drain and place in a warmed dish; cover and keep warm.

3 Cut four 25 cm (10 inch) greaseproof paper squares. Place a mound of spinach on each square. Scatter over a few coriander seeds and the diced shallots. Place 2 sole paupiettes on top. Scatter over the parsley and diced tomato. Season with salt and pepper and top with a knob of butter. Moisten with the fish stock.

4 Fold the greaseproof paper over the filling, sealing in the edges. Place the parcels on a greased baking tray and cook in a preheated oven at 200°C (400°F) mark 6 for 10-15 minutes.

5 Open the parcels and carefully transfer the contents to warmed serving plates. Spoon the rice into warmed greased dariole moulds. Press down, then turn out onto the plates. Serve at once.

Monkfish with Lemon and Caperberry Vinaigrette

450 g (1 lb) filleted monkfish, skinned
grated zest and juice of 1 lemon
30 ml (2 tbsp) mixed black and pink
   peppercorns
30 ml (2 tbsp) plain flour
5 ml (1 tsp) salt
60 ml (4 tbsp) olive oil

Lemon and Caperberry Vinaigrette:
90 ml (3 fl oz) olive oil
grated zest of 1 large lemon
45 ml (3 tbsp) lemon juice
30 ml (2 tbsp) caper berries
1 shallot, finely chopped

To Garnish:
lemon slices

1 Cut the fish into 2 cm (¾ inch) thick rounds. Lay in a shallow dish, sprinkle with the lemon juice and leave to marinate for 10 minutes, or longer if possible.

2 Crush the mixed peppercorns, using a pestle and mortar. Mix with the flour, salt and lemon zest. Spread the seasoned flour on a plate.

3 Pat the fish dry with kitchen paper, then coat with the seasoned flour.

4 Heat the oil in a heavy-based frying pan until hot. Fry the fish in two batches. Add to the hot oil and cook for 2-3 minutes on each side; keep the first batch warm while cooking the second.

5 Meanwhile make the vinaigrette. Put the oil, lemon zest and juice in a screw-topped jar and shake well to combine. Add the caper berries, and a little salt if needed.

6 Add the second batch of cooked fish to the first; keep warm. Add the shallot to the pan with a little more oil if necessary and fry quickly over a high heat for 30 seconds. Pour the dressing into the pan and let it bubble to reduce slightly, whisking briefly.

7 Arrange the fish on warmed serving plates. Garnish with lemon slices and surround with the hot vinaigrette.

Note: Jars of caper berries are available from delicatessens and some larger supermarkets.

Quail Terrine with Morello Cherries and Madeira

450 g (1 lb) streaky bacon
6 quail breasts
salt and freshly ground black pepper
15 ml (1 tbsp) walnut oil
345 g (12 oz) chicken livers
1 shallot, finely chopped
30 ml (2 tbsp) chopped tarragon
45 ml (3 tbsp) Madeira
1 egg
60 ml (4 tbsp) French Morello cherries,
  preserved in syrup
salt and freshly ground black pepper

To Serve:
salad leaves
cherry or cranberry sauce (optional)

1 Line the base and sides of a greased 450 g (1 lb) loaf tin with the bacon rashers, leaving sufficient overhanging the sides to cover the top of the finished terrine. Set aside. Season the quail breasts with salt and pepper and sprinkle with the walnut oil; set aside.

2 Put the chicken livers, shallot, tarragon, 15 ml (1 tbsp) Madeira and the egg in a food processor and work until smooth.

3 Meanwhile place the cherries and remaining 30 ml (2 tbsp) Madeira in a saucepan and heat gently for 3 minutes.

4 Pour half of the chicken liver mixture into the prepared tin and layer half of the cherry mixture on top. Arrange the quail breasts on top and cover with the rest of the cherries. Pour the rest of the chicken liver mixture over the cherries. Fold over the bacon, then cover with foil.

5 Stand the loaf tin in a roasting tin, containing a 5 cm (2 inch) depth of water. Bake in a preheated oven at 180°C (350°F) mark 4 for 1-1½ hours, until cooked through. Leave to cool in the tin, then unmould and slice.

6 Serve the terrine slices on a bed of salad leaves, accompanied by a warmed cherry or cranberry sauce if desired.

Devilled Chicken Livers with Walnuts on a Mixed Leaf Salad

225 g (8 oz) chicken livers
45 ml (3 tbsp) Worcestershire sauce
5 ml (1 tsp) cayenne pepper
5 ml (1 tsp) powdered mustard
salt and freshly ground black pepper
50 g (2 oz) walnuts, coarsely chopped
a little walnut oil
15 ml (1 tbsp) light olive oil flavoured with garlic and chilli
5 ml (1 tsp) unsalted butter

Salad:
sufficient mixed salad leaves for 4 (eg lamb's lettuce, rocket)

Lime Vinaigrette:
30 ml (2 tbsp) olive oil (see note)
15 ml (1 tbsp) freshly squeezed lime juice
5 ml (1 tsp) thin honey
2.5 ml (½ tsp) powdered mustard
salt and freshly ground pepper

1 Trim the chicken livers of any fibrous parts, then cut each one into 3 even-sized pieces; set aside.

2 For the marinade, put the Worcestershire sauce in a small bowl and whisk in the cayenne, mustard and seasoning. Add the chicken livers, turn to coat with the marinade, then cover and leave to marinate in the refrigerator for about 2 hours.

3 Toss the walnuts in a little walnut oil until well coated, then spread on a baking tray and toast in a preheated oven at 200°C (400°F) mark 6 for 5-10 minutes. Drain on kitchen paper and allow to cool.

4 Combine the salad leaves in a bowl. Put all the ingredients for the lime vinaigrette in a small screw-topped jar and shake well until amalgamated. Pour the dressing over the salad leaves and toss to coat.

5 Drain the chicken livers. Heat the garlic and chilli flavoured oil with the butter in a heavy-based frying pan. Toss in the chicken livers and cook over a moderately high heat for a few minutes, moving them gently with a spatula, until firm and browned all over, but still pink in the centre. Add half of the walnuts and toss to mix.

6 Arrange the dressed salad leaves on individual serving plates. Spoon the hot chicken livers on top and sprinkle over the reserved walnuts. Serve at once.

Note: Keep a jar of light olive oil flavoured with chives, rosemary, marjoram and the zest of 1 lime, to use for the base of this salad dressing.

Lemon Risotto with Fresh Herb Salad

15 ml (1 tbsp) oil
75 g (3 oz) butter
4 shallots, finely chopped
600 ml (1 pint) chicken stock (homemade)
salt and freshly ground black pepper
150 g (5 oz) carnaroli or Arborio rice
50 g (2 oz) Parmesan cheese, freshly grated
30 ml (2 tbsp) chopped herbs (eg basil,
  chives, thyme, parsley, rocket, sorrel)
dash of Noilly Prat

Fresh Herb Salad:
30 ml (2 tbsp) walnut oil
15 ml (1 tbsp) olive oil
15 ml (1 tbsp) blackberry vinegar
5 ml (1 tsp) red wine vinegar
5 ml (1 tsp) balsamic vinegar
50 g (2 oz) assorted herb leaves (eg rocket,
  baby spinach, sorrel, basil, parsley)

To Serve:
Parmesan Tuiles (see right)

1 Heat the oil with half of the butter in a medium heavy-based pan. Add the shallots and sauté until soft and translucent; do not allow to brown. In the meantime, bring the chicken stock almost to the boil in another pan, season, lower the heat and keep at simmering point.

2 Add the rice to the shallots and stir over the heat for 1-2 minutes until the grains are coated with the butter and oil, and shiny. Add a ladleful of chicken stock and cook, stirring constantly, until all the liquid is absorbed. Continue adding the stock, a ladleful at a time, ensuring each addition is absorbed before adding the next, until the rice is *al dente* (cooked but firm to the bite). This should take approximately 18-20 minutes.

3 Add the remaining butter, cheese, herbs and Noilly Prat. Stir gently.

4 For the salad, combine the oils and vinegars in a screw-topped jar with seasoning to taste and shake vigorously to combine. Just before serving, toss the herb leaves in the dressing to coat.

5 Serve the risotto with the herb salad and Parmesan Tuiles.

Parmesan Tuiles

50 g (2 oz) Parmesan cheese, coarsely grated

1 Place a sheet of non-stick baking parchment on a baking tray and sprinkle the cheese into oval shapes on the paper. Cook in a preheated oven at 180°C (350°F) mark 4 for about 5 minutes until the cheese melts and turns golden brown.

2 Carefully remove with a spatula and lift over a rolling pin. Leave until cool and crisp, then transfer to an airtight tin to store until needed.

Leek and Goat's Cheese Ravioli with Gremolata

Pasta Dough:
150 g (5 oz) durum wheat flour
50 g (2 oz) strong plain flour
pinch of salt
2 eggs (size 3)
2 egg yolks (size 3)

Filling:
2 large leeks (white and tender green parts only), cleaned
25 g (1 oz) unsalted butter
salt and freshly ground black pepper
freshly grated nutmeg
100 g (3½ oz) skinless chicken breast fillet
pinch of ground mace
1 small egg white (size 4 or 5)
150 ml (¼ pint) double cream
200 g (7 oz) firm goat's cheese

Gremolata:
handful of flat-leaf parsley, finely chopped
grated zest of 1 lemon
sea salt

To Finish:
beaten egg yolk, for brushing
flour, for dusting
75 g (3 oz) butter

1 To make the pasta dough, put the flours, salt, eggs and egg yolks in a food processor (or bowl of a mixer). Using the dough blade (or hook), work to a smooth, elastic ball of dough, adding a little water or more flour if necessary. Cover the bowl with a damp tea-towel and leave to rest.

2 To prepare the filling, finely slice the leeks. Heat the butter in a pan, add the leeks and sweat for about 5 minutes until softened. Season with salt, pepper and a little grated nutmeg. Let cool completely.

3 Cut the chicken into small pieces and place in a food processor. Add 5 ml (1 tsp) salt, some pepper and the ground mace. Process to a fine purée. Chill the mixture in the refrigerator for 15-20 minutes. Return to the processor and gradually work in the egg white, then the cream, using the pulse button if possible. It is important to avoid overworking the mousseline or it may separate. Pass through a fine sieve into a bowl. Add the cooled leeks, then crumble in the goat's cheese and mix well. Cover and refrigerate until needed.

4 Roll out the dough in manageable portions, using a pasta machine, keeping the rest of the dough wrapped. Pass the dough through the machine on its widest setting, then fold the dough and pass through the machine repeatedly, narrowing the setting by one notch each time until you reach the thinnest setting. Cut the sheets of pasta into 6.5 cm (2½ inch) squares; you will need about 32 in total.

5 Place a heaped teaspoonful of the filling in the centre of half of the pasta squares. Brush the edges of the pasta with a little egg yolk and cover with the remaining pasta squares. Pinch the edges together to seal and dust the ravioli with flour.

6 To make the gremolata, mix the chopped parsley with the grated lemon zest and season with a little sea salt.

7 Add the ravioli to a large pan of well-salted lightly boiling water and cook for about 7 minutes. Drain thoroughly.

8 Meanwhile, melt the butter in a frying pan large enough to hold all the ravioli, adding 15-30 ml (1-2 tbsp) water to form an emulsion. Stir in the gremolata and add the ravioli. Warm through, ensuring all the ravioli are coated with the melted butter and gremolata. Serve immediately.

Double Baked Onion Soufflé with a Truffle Oil Dressing

25 g (1 oz) butter
½ onion, finely diced
25 g (1 oz) plain flour
150 ml (¼ pint) milk
salt and freshly ground black pepper
3 eggs (size 3), separated
15 g (½ oz) freshly grated Parmesan cheese

Truffle Oil Dressing:
150 ml (¼ pint) vegetable stock
15 ml (1 tbsp) butter
15 ml (1 tbsp) plain flour
150 ml (¼ pint) whipping cream
15 ml (1 tbsp) truffle oil

To Serve:
20 ml (4 tsp) chopped black olives
20 ml (4 tsp) scented geranium jelly
20 ml (4 tsp) herb mustard

1 Melt the butter in a saucepan, add the onion and sauté gently until softened. Add the flour and cook, stirring, for 1 minute. Gradually stir in the milk and cook, stirring, until thickened and smooth. Season with salt and pepper to taste. Remove from the heat and stir in the beaten egg yolks.

2 In a separate bowl, whisk the egg whites until stiff peaks form, then carefully fold into the onion mixture, retaining as much air as possible.

3 Lightly grease 4 ramekins and coat with the Parmesan cheese. Divide the soufflé mixture between the ramekins. Stand them in a shallow baking tin containing enough boiling water to come half-way up the sides of the dishes.

4 Bake in a preheated oven at 180°C (350°F) mark 4 for about 5 minutes until risen and golden. Allow to cool, then turn out; set aside until ready to serve.

5 To make the truffle oil dressing, bring the stock to the boil in a saucepan. Meanwhile, mix the butter and flour together to form a beurre manié. Whisk into the stock, a piece at a time, then add the cream and bring to the boil. Boil steadily to reduce by about half and concentrate the flavour. Stir in the truffle oil.

6 When ready to serve, place the soufflés in individual gratin dishes. Pour over the truffle oil dressing and bake in the oven for 4-5 minutes. Dress each serving with a teaspoonful each of black olives, scented geranium jelly and herb mustard.

Beetroot Mousse with Horseradish Sauce

Beetroot Mousse:
150 ml (¼ pint) vegetable stock
½ sachet powdered gelatine
225 g (8 oz) beetroot, cooked and peeled
juice and grated rind of ½ lemon
5 ml (1 tsp) balsamic vinegar
5 ml (1 tsp) sugar
salt and freshly ground black pepper
150 ml (¼ pint) whipping cream

Horseradish Sauce:
30 ml (2 tbsp) grated fresh horseradish root
10 ml (2 tsp) lemon juice
10 ml (2 tsp) sugar
pinch of powdered mustard
150 ml (¼ pint) double cream

To Garnish:
salad leaves

1 To make the beetroot mousse, warm the vegetable stock in a small pan over a low heat until hot but not boiling, then sprinkle the powdered gelatine over the surface. Allow the gelatine to dissolve completely, then remove from the heat and allow to cool slightly.

2 Put the beetroot, lemon rind and juice, balsamic vinegar and sugar in a food processor and work to a smooth purée. Add the cooled gelatine mixture, salt and pepper, and process briefly until evenly mixed. Cool until just beginning to set.

3 Lightly whip the cream and fold into the beetroot mixture. Check the seasoning. Pour into lightly greased ramekins and chill in the refrigerator until set.

4 To make the horseradish sauce, mix together the horseradish, lemon juice, sugar and mustard. Whip the cream until soft peaks form, then fold into the horseradish mixture.

5 To serve, turn the mousses out onto individual serving plates. Drizzle the horseradish sauce around the mousses and garnish with salad leaves.

Griddled Asparagus and Leeks with Pecorino, on a bed of Socca

12 small leeks
12 asparagus spears
olive oil, for brushing
50 g (2 oz) pecorino Romano cheese, freshly grated
30 ml (2 tbsp) lemon juice

Socca:
75 g (3 oz) gram (chickpea) flour
sea salt and freshly ground black pepper
300 ml (½ pint) water
7.5 ml (1½ tsp) olive oil

1 First make the socca. Put the gram flour into a mixing bowl and season liberally with salt and pepper. Add the water, mixing gently until smooth. Add the oil and beat briefly to emulsify, then pour into a greased baking tin measuring about 23 x 15 cm (9 x 6 inches), to give a depth of about 5 mm (¼ inch). Bake in the top of a preheated oven at 240°C (475°F) mark 9 for about 20 minutes or until the socca is firm.

2 When cool enough to handle, cut four 7.5 cm (3 inch) rounds from the socca and transfer to a wire rack to cool.

3 Preheat a ridged griddle over a medium heat. Brush with oil, then arrange the leeks and asparagus in a single layer on the griddle. Brush the vegetables with oil. Cook for about 5 minutes, turning occasionally and brushing with more oil. When almost but not quite cooked, sprinkle with two thirds of the cheese and the lemon juice. Cook for a further 1 minute.

4 In the meantime, brush the socca rounds with olive oil and place under a preheated moderate grill for about 1 minute to heat through. Sprinkle with the remaining cheese.

5 To serve, place a round of socca in the centre of each warmed serving plate and arrange the leeks and asparagus on top. Serve at once.

Tarte à l' Oignon

Sweet red onions are used for these rich, creamy individual flans. It is important to fry them very slowly until completely soft before filling the flan cases.

Pastry:
175 g (6 oz) plain flour
3 large pinches of salt
75 ml (5 tbsp) extra-virgin olive oil
2 cloves garlic, crushed
7.5 ml (1½ tsp) water

Filling:
65 ml (4½ tbsp) extra-virgin olive oil
2 medium red onions, halved and sliced
15 ml (1 tbsp) balsamic vinegar
15 ml (1 tbsp) caster sugar
250 m (8 fl oz) double cream
1 egg (size 2)
2 egg yolks (size 2)
salt and freshly ground black pepper

To Garnish:
basil leaves

1 To make the pastry, sift the flour and salt into a bowl. Heat the olive oil in a pan, add the garlic and water and heat until it begins to bubble, then gradually mix into the flour.

2 Divide the dough into 4 portions and use to line 4 greased 10 cm (4 inch) individual flan tins, pressing the dough against the sides and base with your fingers. Chill in the refrigerator for about 30 minutes.

3 Bake in a preheated oven at 220°C (425°F) mark 7 for 10 minutes. Remove from the oven and lower the oven setting to 190°C (375°F) mark 5.

4 For the filling, heat the olive oil in a heavy-based frying pan over a low heat. Add the onions, balsamic vinegar and sugar and cook slowly, stirring frequently, until the onions are soft.

5 In a mixing bowl, whisk together the cream, whole egg, egg yolks and seasoning. Stir in the cooked onions.

6 Spoon the onion filling into the pastry cases and cook in the centre of the oven for 15 minutes or until lightly golden brown. Serve garnished with basil leaves.

Mixed Herb Salad with Quail's Eggs

12 quail's eggs
salt and freshly ground black pepper
50 g (2 oz) piece Parmesan cheese
30 ml (2 tbsp) virgin olive oil
50 g (2 oz) very thinly sliced pancetta, cut into strips
1 clove garlic, crushed
15 ml (1 tbsp) basil oil
15 ml (1 tbsp) balsamic vinegar
2.5 ml (½ tsp) caster sugar
sufficient mixed salad leaves to serve 4 (eg lamb's lettuce, frisée, radicchio)
few mixed herb leaves (eg basil, flat-leaved parsley, dill)

1 Cook the quail's eggs in a pan of boiling salted water for approximately 5 minutes. Drain and cool under running cold water until cold. Peel the eggs and halve lengthwise; set aside.

2 Thinly pare the Parmesan into shavings, using a potato peeler.

3 Heat 15 ml (1 tbsp) olive oil in a small non-stick frying pan. Add the pancetta and garlic and fry until crispy. Drain on kitchen paper.

4 For the dressing, whisk together the basil oil, remaining olive oil, balsamic vinegar, seasoning and sugar thoroughly.

5 Place the salad leaves and herbs in a large bowl, pour over the dressing and toss to coat the leaves thoroughly.

6 Divide the salad between 4 serving plates, arrange the halved quail's eggs around the edge and sprinkle the pancetta and fried garlic over the middle of the salad. Top with the wafer-thin shavings of Parmesan. Serve immediately.

Warm Goat's Cheese with Apple and Celeriac Salad

4 mature goat's cheeses (preferably Crottin de
   Chauvignole)
30 ml (2 tbsp) flour, for dusting
1 egg, lightly beaten
90 ml (6 tbsp) slivered almonds
olive oil, for frying

Salad:
¼ small celeriac, peeled
1 tart dessert apple (eg Granny Smith)
1 small cos or sweet Romaine lettuce
handful of rocket leaves

Dressing:
7.5 ml (1½ tsp) hazelnut oil
45 ml (3 tbsp) sunflower oil
22 ml (1½ tbsp) cider vinegar
large pinch of salt
2-3 grinds of black pepper

Bread Croûtes:
4 slices French country-style bread
15 g (½ oz) butter

1 Lightly dust the goat's cheeses with flour. Dip into the beaten egg, then coat with the almonds. Place on a flat plate, cover and chill in the refrigerator until needed.

2 Cut the celeriac into fine julienne and immerse in a bowl of cold water acidulated with a squeeze of lemon juice. Peel, halve and core the apple; cut into julienne and add to the acidulated water.

3 For the bread croûtes, cut a round from each slice of bread just larger than the cheese. Heat the butter in a frying pan, add the bread slices and fry until golden on both sides. Drain on kitchen paper and keep warm.

4 Heat a thin film of olive oil in a frying pan, add the cheeses and fry gently for 1-2 minutes, turning carefully until coloured on all sides. Transfer to an oiled baking sheet and roast in a preheated oven at 200°C (400°F) mark 6 for about 3 minutes.

5 Meanwhile, whisk together the ingredients for the dressing. Roughly tear the salad leaves. Drain the celeriac and apple julienne and pat dry with kitchen paper. Toss the salad leaves and julienne separately with the dressing.

6 Arrange the salad leaves in the centre of each serving plate. Surround with the celeriac and apple julienne. Place each cheese on a bread croûte and position on the salad leaves. Serve at once.

Salad of Cooked Peppers with a Saffron Vinaigrette

3 green peppers
2 red peppers
80 ml (5 tbsp) olive oil
2.5 ml (½ tsp) ground cumin
2 cloves garlic, peeled
2 ripe, red plum tomatoes, skinned, seeded
 and roughly chopped
salt and freshly ground black pepper

Saffron Vinaigrette:
45 ml (3 tbsp) olive oil
small pinch of saffron threads
1 clove garlic, peeled
5 ml (1 tsp) wine vinegar
45 ml (3 tbsp) water
large pinch of salt
small pinch of cayenne pepper
pinch of sugar

Deep-fried Coriander:
24 coriander leaves
corn oil for deep-frying

To Garnish:
1 small tomato, skinned, seeded and finely
 chopped

1 Grill the peppers under a preheated hot grill, turning occasionally, until blistered and charred all over. Place in a bowl, cover and leave to cool; the steam created will help to lift the skins. Peel away the skins, then halve, core and cut the peppers into 1 cm (½ inch) wide strips.

2 Heat the olive oil in a saucepan. Add the pepper strips and cumin, and cook, stirring, for 1 minute. Add the garlic, tomatoes and seasoning. Simmer for 20 minutes, until the peppers are very tender. Leave to cool, then check the seasoning.

3 To make the saffron vinaigrette, heat the olive oil in a small pan, add the saffron and garlic, cover and sweat for about 1 minute. Add the vinegar, water, salt, cayenne and sugar. Remove from the heat and leave to cool and infuse for at least 30 minutes. Discard the garlic and check the seasoning.

4 Just before serving, prepare the deep-fried coriander. Wash the coriander leaves and pat dry thoroughly on kitchen paper. Heat the oil in a deep-fat fryer to 165°C (325°F), then add the coriander leaves. Deep-fry until the leaves stop bubbling. Remove with a slotted spoon and drain on kitchen paper.

5 Remove the garlic and as much cooking oil as possible from the cooked peppers. Pile a mound of peppers onto the centre of each serving plate. Drizzle the vinaigrette around them and scatter the diced tomato on the vinaigrette. Garnish with the deep-fried coriander.

Double Tomato Tartlets

Pastry:
100 g (4 oz) plain flour, sifted
pinch of salt
50 g (2 oz) unsalted butter, diced
2 egg yolks
*15 ml (1 tbsp) oil, from the sun-dried
  tomato jar*

Filling:
4 cherry tomatoes
5 ml (1 tsp) salt
175 g (6 oz) mascarpone
75 g (3 oz) Jarlsberg cheese, grated
90 ml (6 tbsp) chopped basil leaves
salt and freshly ground black pepper
*4 sun-dried tomatoes in oil, well drained
  and halved*

To Serve:
a little oil from the sun-dried tomato jar

1 To make the pastry, place the flour, salt and butter in a food processor and work until the mixture resembles breadcrumbs. Mix the egg yolks and oil together; add to the rubbed-in mixture. Process briefly until the dough binds together, adding 1 or 2 drops of cold water, if necessary.

2 Wrap the dough in cling film and leave to rest in the refrigerator for 30 minutes.

3 Roll out the pastry thinly and use to line four 9 cm (3½ inch) lightly buttered tartlet tins (preferably loose-based ones). Prick the pastry bases with a fork and chill in the refrigerator for 20 minutes. (This pastry is 'short' so it may crack.)

4 Meanwhile, prepare the filling. Slice the cherry tomatoes into rounds, sprinkle with a little salt and place on a wire rack over kitchen paper. Cover with kitchen paper and leave to drain for 20 minutes; pat dry.

5 Place the mascarpone, Jarlsberg and half of the chopped basil in the food processor. Add seasoning and process until smooth and creamy.

6 Line the pastry cases with greaseproof paper and baking beans and bake in a preheated oven at 200°C (400°F) mark 6 for 10 minutes. Remove from the oven and let cool. Lower the oven setting to 180°C (350°F) mark 4.

7 Divide the cheese mixture between the pastry cases. Arrange a line of fresh tomato slices across the middle and put a sun-dried tomato half on either side. Season with pepper.

8 Place on a baking tray and bake in the oven for about 30 minutes, until the filling is set and golden brown. Leave to stand for 10 minutes.

9 Carefully remove the tartlets from the tins and place on warmed serving plates. Surround with the remaining chopped basil leaves, and drizzle with a little sun-dried tomato oil. Serve warm.

Polenta with Home-dried Tomatoes, Mozzarella, Basil and Olive Tapenade

Polenta:
100 g (3½ oz) quick-cook (instant) polenta
500 ml (16 fl oz) water
salt and freshly ground black pepper
75 g (3 oz) pecorino cheese, grated
knob of butter

Filling:
1 buffalo mozzarella cheese, about 125 g
  (4 oz)
8 home-dried tomato halves (see below)
handful of basil leaves

Tapenade:
125 g (4 oz) black olives (pitted)
1 clove garlic, peeled
2 canned anchovy fillets
15 ml (1 tbsp) extra-virgin olive oil
5 ml (1 tsp) lemon juice

1 To cook the polenta, bring the water to the boil in a large saucepan. Add 2.5 ml (½ tsp) salt. Sprinkle in the polenta, whisking constantly. Lower the heat and cook, stirring continuously, for 5 minutes, until the polenta is smooth and very thick; it will leave the side of the pan. Add the grated cheese and knob of butter. Stir until evenly amalgamated.

2 Spread the polenta thinly on a baking tray, as evenly as possible, to a depth of about 5 mm (¼ inch). Leave to cool and set.

3 For the filling, chop the mozzarella, tomatoes and basil and combine in a bowl. Drizzle over a little olive oil (from the tomatoes) and set aside to infuse.

4 To make the tapenade, put the olives, garlic and anchovies in a blender or food processor and process until finely chopped. Add the olive oil and lemon juice and process until evenly mixed. Season with salt and pepper to taste.

5 When ready serve, cut the polenta into 5 cm (2 inch) squares, using a ravioli cutter or pastry cutter. Brown under a preheated grill on both sides. Sandwich the polenta squares together in pairs with the mozzarella and tomato filling.

Home-dried Tomatoes: Halve 16 ripe plum tomatoes lengthwise, then scoop out and discard the seeds and hard cores. Lay the tomato halves on 2 baking sheets and drizzle with 60 ml (4 tbsp) olive oil. Sprinkle with 15 ml (1 tbsp) sugar and 5 ml (1 tsp) salt. Bake in the oven on the lowest possible setting – 50°C (100°F) mark ⅛ for about 12-14 hours until crinkly. The tomatoes will be drier than sun-dried tomatoes and have a more intense flavour. They can be used straight away or stored in olive oil.

41

Black Pudding en Croûte with Mulberry dressed Salad Leaves

40 g (1½ oz) butter
2 leeks, trimmed (white parts only), chopped
1 clove garlic, crushed
½ large potato, peeled and diced
2 apples, (preferably Granny Smith)
225 g (8 oz) black pudding (see note), diced
15 ml (1 tbsp) apache jelly (see note)
15 ml (1 tbsp) thyme jelly (see note)
salt and freshly ground black pepper
3 sheets filo pastry
a little melted butter, for brushing
15 ml (1 tbsp) Calvados

Salad:
sufficient mixed salad leaves for 4, (eg
  rocket, radicchio, oak leaf lettuce)

Dressing:
60 ml (4 tbsp) hazelnut oil
30 ml (2 tbsp) groundnut oil
30 ml (2 tbsp) mulberry or raspberry wine
  vinegar
5 ml (1 tsp) wholegrain mustard
5 ml (1 tsp) red wine vinegar

1 Heat 25 g (1 oz) of the butter in a frying pan, add the leeks, garlic and potato and sauté until softened. In the meantime, peel, core and dice 1 apple. Add to the pan with the black pudding and cook for 1-2 minutes. Stir in the apache and thyme jellies. Season with salt and pepper. Leave to cool.

2 When the mixture is cool, lay the 3 sheets of filo pastry one on top of the other on a lightly floured surface, then cut four 12 cm (5 inch) squares through the triple thickness.

3 Spoon the black pudding mixture in the centre of each and brush the pastry edges lightly with melted butter. Bring the edges up over the filling and twist together to form 4 purse shapes. Brush with melted butter. Transfer to a baking sheet and bake in a preheated oven at 200°C (400°F) mark 6 for 15-20 minutes until golden brown.

4 Meanwhile, peel, quarter and core the remaining apple. Cut into segments. Melt the remaining butter in a frying pan, add the apple and sauté until golden brown. Add the Calvados and flame. When the flame has died down, remove from the heat; keep warm.

5 Combine the salad leaves in a bowl. Put the ingredients for the dressing in a screw-topped jar and shake vigorously until amalgamated. Pour the dressing over the salad and toss lightly.

6 To serve, place a filo purse in the centre of each serving plate, surround with dressed salad leaves and place 3 or 4 sautéed apple wedges to one side.

Note: It is important to use a good quality black pudding, which is not too fatty.

Apache and thyme flavoured apple jellies are available from specialist shops. If unobtainable, use ordinary apple jelly and flavour with a little chilli sauce and finely chopped fresh thyme leaves.

Fish & Shellfish

Roast Sea Bass with Braised Fennel and a Bloody Mary Sauce

4 sea bass fillets, with skin, each about
   175 g (6 oz)
30 ml (2 tbsp) olive oil
salt and freshly ground black pepper

Bloody Mary Sauce:
8 vine-ripened tomatoes
15 ml (1 tbsp) olive oil
15 ml (1 tbsp) tomato ketchup
15 ml (1 tbsp) vodka
5 ml (1 tsp) Worcestershire sauce
75 g (3 oz) butter, in pieces

Braised Fennel:
4 fennel bulbs, trimmed
5 ml (1 tsp) caster sugar
15 ml (1 tbsp) lemon juice
90 ml (3 fl oz) olive oil

To Garnish:
125 g (4 oz) pitted black olives, finely
   chopped
fennel fronds

1 First make the sauce. Put the tomatoes in a small baking tin and roast in a preheated oven at 180°C (375°F) mark 4 for 40-50 minutes. Let cool slightly, then purée in a blender or food processor. Pass through a sieve into a pan to remove the skins. Heat gently and stir in the olive oil and tomato ketchup, followed by the vodka and Worcestershire sauce; set aside.

2 Meanwhile, prepare the fennel. Halve the fennel bulbs lengthwise and place in a casserole. Sprinkle with the sugar and lemon juice, season with salt and pepper and pour on the olive oil. Cover and cook in a preheated oven at for about 30 minutes until softened. Remove the lid and return to the oven for a further 10 minutes or until lightly browned. Drain off the oil, cover and keep warm.

3 Brush the sea bass fillets with a little of the olive oil and season with salt and pepper. Heat the rest of the oil in a frying pan. Add the sea bass fillets, skin-side down, and cook for 1 minute. Turn the fillets and cook for 1 minute, then turn again and cook for 1 minute longer. Transfer to a preheated oven at 200°C (400°F) mark 6 and cook for 2 minutes. Keep warm.

4 Just before serving, gently reheat the sauce and whisk in the butter, a piece at a time, until fully incorporated. Season with salt and pepper to taste. Place two braised fennel halves in the centre of each serving plate. Position the sea bass on top. Surround with the tomato sauce and garnish with the chopped black olives and fennel fronds. Serve with Aubergine Crisps (see page 97).

Grilled Sea Bass with Fennel Butter and Cucumber Noodles

2 small or 1 large sea bass, about 1.5 kg
(3¼ lb), filleted and skinned
30 ml (2 tbsp) fennel seeds
40 g (1½ oz) unsalted butter, softened
few drops of lemon juice
salt and freshly ground black pepper
a little olive oil, for brushing
30 ml (2 tbsp) Pernod

Cucumber Noodles:
1 cucumber
20 g (¾ oz) unsalted butter
To Garnish:
fennel leaves

1 Remove any residual bones from the fish with tweezers. Cut 4 neat fillets, cover and refrigerate until ready to cook.

2 Grind the fennel seeds to a fine powder, using a pestle and mortar, then pass through a sieve into a bowl. Add the softened butter and a few drops of lemon juice to taste, beating until evenly blended. Chill the fennel butter to firm up, then slice and cut out star shapes, using a pastry cutter. Refrigerate until ready to serve.

3 To prepare the cucumber noodles, peel, halve and deseed the cucumber, then cut into fine julienne. Heat the butter in a frying pan, add the cucumber julienne and cook gently for about 2 minutes. Season with salt and pepper to taste; keep warm.

4 Season the sea bass fillets with salt and pepper and brush lightly with olive oil. Place skinned-side down on a grill rack and cook under a preheated moderate grill for 3-4 minutes without turning, until the flesh is just opaque. Meanwhile, heat a metal skewer over a flame. Sear the fish fillets in a criss-cross pattern with the red hot skewer.

5 Divide the cucumber noodles between warmed serving plates and position the fish fillets on top. Heat the Pernod in a small pan, ignite, then pour over the fish and noodles. Top with the fennel butter and garnish with fennel leaves. Serve at once, with Sautéed Potatoes (see page 102).

Poached Turbot on Creamed Spinach and Tagliatelle, with a Tomato Butter Sauce

4 turbot fillets, each about 175 g (6 oz),
  skinned
juice of ½ lemon
15 ml (1 tbsp) chopped basil leaves
salt and freshly ground black pepper

Pasta:
1 egg (size 4)
110 g (4 oz) strong white bread flour
pinch of salt
15 ml (1 tbsp) virgin olive oil

Roast Tomatoes:
12 firm cherry tomatoes
15 ml (1 tbsp) olive oil

Tomato Sauce:
225 g (8 oz) very ripe tomatoes
25 g (1 oz) unsalted butter, chilled and
  diced
45 ml (3 tbsp) virgin olive oil

Creamed Spinach:
225 g (8 oz) spinach leaves, stalks removed
1 clove garlic, crushed
30 ml (2 tbsp) double cream
freshly grated nutmeg

To Garnish:
basil leaves

1 Line a ceramic baking dish with foil, allowing sufficient foil to overhang the edges generously. Lay the turbot fillets on the foil and sprinkle with the lemon juice and chopped basil leaves. Season lightly. Fold the edges of the foil over the fish and seal to form a parcel. Set aside.

2 To make the pasta, beat the egg in a large bowl, then sift in the flour together with a pinch of salt. Add the olive oil. Mix

together with a fork, then press the dough together with your hands. Transfer to a lightly floured surface and knead the dough for 5-10 minutes until smooth. Wrap in cling film and leave to rest in the refrigerator for 20 minutes.

3 Place the cherry tomatoes in a small roasting tin. Drizzle over the olive oil and season with salt and pepper. Turn the tomatoes to coat with the oil.

4 Unwrap the pasta dough and cut into manageable pieces. Re-wrap all but one piece. Flatten the piece and pass it through the pasta machine on its widest setting. Fold the dough and pass through the machine repeatedly, narrowing the setting by one notch each time until it passes through the second to last notch. Repeat with the remaining dough, then fit the tagliatelle cutters. Pass the pasta sheets through to cut the tagliatelle. Hang to dry on a pasta rack or over the edge of a large mixing bowl for 30 minutes.

5 Bake the foil-wrapped fish and cherry tomatoes in a preheated oven at 190°C (375°F) mark 5 for 20 minutes.

6 Meanwhile, to make the sauce, place the tomatoes in a food processor and process to a pulp. Pass through a sieve to remove the skin and pips. Gently warm the sieved tomato pulp in a saucepan. Whisk in the diced butter, a piece at a time. Add the olive oil and seasoning to taste; keep warm.

7 Place the spinach in a pan with just the water clinging to the leaves after washing and the crushed garlic. Cook over a low heat for 3-5 minutes until the spinach has just wilted. Drain thoroughly and pat dry. Season well with salt and pepper. Add the cream and nutmeg to taste. Chop the spinach and mix well with the cream.

8 Bring a large pan of water to the boil. Add the tagliatelle and cook for 2-4 minutes until *al dente* (tender but firm to the bite); drain thoroughly.

9 To serve, divide the tagliatelle equally between 4 warmed serving plates arranging it in a mound in the middle of each plate. Cover with the spinach, then place a turbot fillet on top. Spoon the tomato sauce around the pasta and place the roasted cherry tomatoes on the sauce. Garnish with basil leaves and serve at once.

Turbot with Leeks and Wild Mushrooms

4 turbot fillets, each about 150 g (5 oz)
75 g (3 oz) butter
6 leeks, white and tender pale green parts
  only, cleaned and chopped
salt and freshly ground black pepper
4 shallots, finely chopped
125 g (4 oz) button mushrooms, finely
  chopped
90 ml (3 fl oz) white wine
25 ml (1 fl oz) Madeira (preferably
  Malmsey)
125 g (4 oz) wild mushrooms (eg trompettes,
  pied de mouton, chanterelles)
60 ml (2 fl oz) chicken stock
10 ml (2 tbsp) tarragon mustard

To Garnish:
dill sprigs

1 Melt 25 g (1 oz) butter in the pan, add the leeks and sauté until soft. Place in a blender and purée until smooth. Season with salt and pepper to taste; keep warm.

2 Melt 15 g (½ oz) butter in the pan, add the shallots and sauté until softened, then add the button mushrooms and cook for a further 1-2 minutes. Add the wine and Madeira and bring to the boil. Transfer to an ovenproof dish.

3 Lay the turbot fillets on top of the shallot and mushroom mixture. Cover the dish and cook in a preheated oven at 180°C (350°F) mark 4 for 8-10 minutes, taking care to avoid overcooking this delicate fish. Leave to rest in a warm place whilst cooking the wild mushrooms.

4 Sauté the wild mushrooms in 15 g (½ oz) butter until tender. Season with salt and pepper to taste.

5 Combine the cooking juices from the fish and the wild mushroom cooking liquor in a pan. Add the chicken stock and bring to the boil. Reduce by one third, then add the tarragon mustard. Whisk in the remaining diced 25 g (1 oz) butter, a piece at a time, then pass through a sieve to remove the shallots and chopped button mushrooms.

6 Season the turbot fillets and warm through if necessary. Place a mound of puréed leeks on each warmed serving plate and lay a turbot fillet on top. Surround with the sauce and scatter the wild mushrooms on top. Garnish with dill and serve with Crispy Potatoes (see page 102).

Steamed Fillets of Red Snapper with Courgettes and Shallots, on a Watercress Sauce

2 courgettes
4 red snapper fillets, each about 175 g (6 oz)
few chives
few parsley sprigs
few thyme sprigs
salt and freshly ground black pepper
30 ml (2 tbsp) unsalted butter
4 shallots, sliced

Watercress Sauce:
small bunch of watercress, stalks removed
20 ml (4 tsp) butter
3 shallots, sliced
30-45 ml (2-3 tbsp) fish stock
15 g (1 tbsp) wine vinegar

1 Trim the courgettes and pare into long strips, using a swivel vegetable peeler. Immerse in a bowl of iced water and place in the refrigerator.

2 To make the watercress sauce, blanch the watercress leaves in a pan of boiling water for 1 minute, then drain and refresh in a bowl of iced water; drain thoroughly. Heat a quarter of the butter in a small pan, add the shallots and sauté until just transparent, then place in a blender with the watercress. Process in short bursts until smooth, adding a little fish stock if necessary. Strain the sauce into a small pan and heat gently, adding just enough stock to give a pouring consistency. Add the wine vinegar and seasoning to taste; set aside.

3 Lay the herbs in a steamer and place the fish fillets on top. Season well and dot with half of the butter. Bring the water in the steamer pan to a gentle boil and position the steamer. Cook for about 8 minutes, depending on the thickness of the fish fillets.

4 Meanwhile, heat the remaining butter in a pan and sauté the shallots until softened. Drain the courgette, pat dry and add to the shallots; cook for 1 minute.

5 Just before serving, gently reheat the sauce and beat in the remaining unsalted butter, a little at a time, until the sauce is glossy and smooth.

6 Spread a pool of watercress sauce on each warmed serving plate and pile the courgette and shallot mixture in the middle. Position the fish fillets on top. Serve at once, accompanied by Cheese and Sesame Tuiles filled with Baby Vegetables (see page 95) and fried potato shavings.

Brill with Mushroom Hollandaise and Herb Sauce

For the herb sauce, you need to prepare a fish stock in advance (see below).

4 fillets of brill, each about 225 g (8 oz), skinned
225 g (8 oz) fresh wild mushrooms, or mixed wild and cultivated
10 ml (2 tsp) truffled sauce or porcini mushroom spread with truffles, or 15 ml (1 tbsp) crème fraîche
salt and freshly ground black pepper
small knob of butter
olive oil, for frying

Herb Sauce:
150 ml (¼ pint) fish stock (see below)
20 ml (4 tsp) chopped thyme
60 ml (4 tbsp) chopped parsley
juice of ½ lemon
20 g (¾ oz) unsalted butter

Hollandaise:
2 egg yolks
15 ml (1 tbsp) water
squeeze of lemon juice, to taste
225 g (8 oz) unsalted butter

1 Finely chop the mushrooms and cook in a dry frying pan, without any fat, over a high heat, until all the liquid from the mushrooms has evaporated. Taste and stir in the truffle sauce or spread if using or, alternatively, the crème fraîche. Season with salt and pepper to taste and set aside in a warm place.

2 Season the fish fillets with salt and pepper. Heat a small knob of butter together with a film of olive oil in a frying pan. Add the fish fillets and fry briefly for about 1 minute on each side to colour. Transfer to a baking sheet and roast in a preheated oven at 230°C (450°F) mark 8 for 10-15 minutes, depending on the thickness of the fillets. Meanwhile, make the herb and hollandaise sauces.

3 For the herb sauce, pour the fish stock into a saucepan and reduce over a high heat by one third. Stir in the herbs, lemon juice and butter. Season with salt and pepper to taste; set aside in a warm place.

4 For the hollandaise, put the egg yolks, water and a squeeze of lemon juice in a blender. Melt the butter in a pan. With the motor running, pour the hot butter through the blender feeder tube in a steady stream. Spoon the hollandaise into a bowl. Gently reheat the mushrooms and fold into the hollandaise. Season with salt and pepper to taste, adding a little extra lemon juice if required.

5 To serve, place a brill fillet in the centre of each warmed serving plate. Pour some of the herb sauce onto the fish and spoon a pool of mushroom hollandaise to one side. Serve immediately, with Stoved New Potatoes (see page 105) and Glazed Green Beans (see page 88).

Fish Stock: Rinse 1.4 kg (3 lb) fish bones under cold running water to remove all traces of blood, then chop roughly. Finely chop 2 leeks, 1 onion, 4 celery sticks (including leaves), ½ head fennel and 2 cloves garlic. Place in a large saucepan and add a small wine glass of Noilly Prat. Boil rapidly until nearly all of the liquid has evaporated. Add the fish bones and 1.8 litres (3 pints) water. Bring to the boil and skim to remove any scum. Add 10 black peppercorns, a handful of parsley stalks and 2 thyme sprigs. Simmer gently for 20 minutes. Strain through a fine sieve.

Cod Fillets wrapped in Parma Ham, with Roasted Peppers, Tomatoes and Aubergines

2 large potatoes
50 g (2 oz) butter (approximately)
salt and freshly ground black pepper
1 large onion, finely sliced
200 g (7 oz) pork caul
4 thick pieces cod fillet, each about 175 g
    (6 oz), skinned
8 slices Parma ham
5 orange peppers
5 yellow peppers
about 200 ml (7 fl oz) olive oil flavoured
    with garlic and thyme (see right)
12 large plum tomatoes, skinned, seeded
    and quartered
1 aubergine
30 ml (2 tbsp) balsamic vinegar
30 ml (2 tbsp) chopped fresh basil
salt and freshly ground black pepper

1 Peel and finely slice the potatoes. Heat 25 g (1 oz) butter in a pan, add the potato slices and sauté gently until soft but not coloured; drain on kitchen paper and season with salt and pepper. Add the onion to the pan, with a little more butter if needed and sauté in the same way. Drain and season.

2 Wash the pig's caul well and squeeze out all the water. Spread it out flat on a clean surface and cut into 4 squares.

3 Season the cod fillets. Lay each one on two overlapping slices of Parma ham and place a layer of onion and a layer of potato on each piece of fish. Wrap the Parma ham around the fish fillet and topping to enclose, then wrap each parcel in a square

of caul. Cover and set aside in the refrigerator.

4 Put the peppers in a shallow roasting tins and drizzle over 90 ml (3 fl oz) of the flavoured olive oil. Roast in a preheated oven at 200°C (400°F) mark 6 for 30-40 minutes until tender, but still slightly retaining their shape. Place the peppers in a bowl and cover tightly with cling film. Pour the oil remaining in the roasting tin into a bowl; set aside.

5 When cool enough to handle, skin, halve and deseed the peppers, adding any juices to the reserved oil. Cut the flesh into large strips. Season with salt and pepper and set aside in a warm place.

6 Put the tomatoes in a shallow roasting tin and drizzle over 45 ml (1½ fl oz) of the flavoured oil. Roast in the oven for 10-15 minutes, making sure they retain some firmness. Season with salt and pepper; set aside in a warm place. Add any oil remaining in the roasting tin to the reserved pepper juices and oil.

7 Heat 30 ml (2 tbsp) flavoured olive oil in a non-stick frying pan with the remaining 25 g (1 oz) butter. Add the cod parcels and fry gently for 3-4 minutes, until golden brown on all sides. Transfer to an oiled baking sheet and bake in the oven for about 8 minutes until the fish is tender.

8 Meanwhile, dice the aubergine. Heat 30 ml (1 fl oz) of the flavoured olive oil in a non-stick frying pan. Add the diced aubergine and fry until golden. Drain on kitchen paper. Season with salt and pepper and keep warm.

9 Just before serving, gently heat the peppers and tomatoes with the reserved juices and oil, an extra 20 ml (4 tsp) of the

flavoured oil and the balsamic vinegar. Stir in the chopped basil. Spoon these vegetables onto warmed serving plates, place the fish on top and scatter the aubergine around. Serve at once.

Flavoured Olive Oil: To prepare this, steep 2 garlic cloves and 6 thyme sprigs in approximately 200 ml (7 fl oz) olive oil in a jar. Seal and leave to infuse overnight or for several days if possible.

Cod and Coriander on a bed of Leeks with Parmesan

*4 thick pieces of cod fillet, each about 150 g
  (5 oz)*
salt and freshly ground black pepper
flour, for coating
15 ml (1 tbsp) butter
25 ml (1 fl oz) olive oil
25 g (1 oz) chopped coriander leaves

Leeks with Parmesan:

olive oil, for cooking
*225 g (8 oz) leeks, trimmed and roughly
  chopped*
50 g (2 oz) Parmesan cheese, freshly grated

To Serve:

Saffron Mash (see page 105)

To Garnish:

roasted red pepper diamonds (see note)
coriander leaves

1 Season the cod fillets with salt and pepper, and coat evenly with flour.

2 Melt the butter in a non-stick frying pan, then add the olive oil. Add the cod fillets with the coriander and pan-fry over a high heat for about 10 minutes until golden brown on both sides, turning the fish halfway through cooking.

3 Meanwhile, cover the base of another frying pan with a thin layer of olive oil. Add the leeks, and season with salt and pepper. Fry gently for about 5 minutes; the leeks should still be slightly crunchy. Add the grated Parmesan and toss to mix.

4 To serve, arrange a ring of roasted red pepper diamonds around the edge of each warned serving plate. Place a mound of Saffron Mash in the centre and top with the leeks. Place the pan-fried fish on the top and garnish with coriander leaves. Serve at once.

Note: To prepare the garnish, cut 1 large red pepper into quarters and place on a baking tray. Sprinkle with sea salt and drizzle with olive oil. Bake in a preheated oven at 180°C (350°F) mark 4 for 1 hour. Remove from the oven and cover with a tea-towel. When cool enough to handle, peel away the skin and cut the flesh into diamonds.

Smoked Salmon and Cod Parcels, with Roast Red Peppers, Tomato and Samphire

4 cod fillets, each about 100 g (3½ oz)
1 large thick slice smoked salmon, about
* 2 mm (¹⁄₁₀ inch) thick*

Cod Marinade:
30 ml (2 tbsp) olive oil
2 rosemary sprigs
4 basil leaves
freshly ground black pepper

Smoked Salmon Marinade:
30 ml (2 tbsp) olive oil
15 ml (1 tbsp) chopped dill
freshly ground black pepper

Stock:
fish trimmings (from cod)
400 ml (14 fl oz) water
4 tomatoes, seeded and chopped
2 shallots, chopped
1 clove garlic, crushed
60 ml (2 fl oz) dry white wine
6 basil leaves, shredded
30 ml (2 tbsp) olive oil (approximately)
salt and freshly ground black pepper
squeeze of lemon juice

To Assemble:
2 red peppers
8 basil leaves
3 tomatoes, skinned, seeded and cut into
* segments*
50 g (2 oz) samphire
4 rosemary sprigs
1 egg, beaten

1 Cut the slice of smoked salmon into 4 pieces, to fit over the cod fillets, then place the salmon and cod in two separate shallow dishes. Add the respective marinade ingredients, turn the fish to coat and leave to marinate at room temperature for at least 1 hour.

2 To make the stock, put the fish trimmings in a saucepan with the water, tomatoes, shallots, garlic, white wine and basil. Bring to the boil, lower the heat and simmer for about 10 minutes. Strain through a fine sieve into a clean pan, then boil to reduce to about 120 ml (4 fl oz). Whisk in sufficient olive oil to counter the bitterness in the juices. Season with a little salt and pepper and add a squeeze of lemon juice. Allow to cool.

3 Place the red peppers under a preheated hot grill and grill, turning frequently, until the skins are blackened and blistered all over. Place in a bowl, cover and leave until cool, then peel away the skins. Halve and deseed the peppers, then cut into strips, about 3 x 1 cm (1¼ x ½ inch).

4 Lay 4 sheets of greaseproof paper on the work surface. Arrange the strips of red pepper on each to form a bed for the fish. Moisten with a little of the stock. Place a cod fillet on each bed of peppers and top with 2 basil leaves. Lay the smoked salmon on top of the cod and arrange alternating stripes of tomato and samphire on top of this. Place a sprig of rosemary next to the fish. Brush the edges of the greaseproof paper with beaten egg and fold the paper over the fish to seal and form parcels.

5 Place on a lightly oiled baking tray and bake in a preheated oven at 220°C (425°F) mark 7 for 11 minutes.

6 Transfer the fish parcels to warmed serving plates and spoon around the cooking juices. Serve with Individual Potatoes Dauphinoise (see page 103) and Green Beans in Minted Vinaigrette (see page 88).

Salmon Parcels with Lime and Coriander Beurre Blanc

For this recipe, the salmon must be taken from the centre of the fish; it should be approximately 10 cm (4 inches) across.

900 g (2 lb) portion filleted salmon (see above)

Stuffing:
2 leeks
1 courgette
2 carrots
salt and freshly ground black pepper

Beurre Blanc:
50 g (2 oz) shallots, peeled and very finely diced
30 ml (2 tbsp) wine vinegar
90 ml (3 fl oz) dry white wine
finely pared zest and juice of 1 lime
15 ml (1 tbsp) whipping cream
225 g (8 oz) unsalted butter, diced
5 ml (1 tsp) ground coriander
salt and freshly ground black pepper

1 Remove the skin from the salmon and pull out any small residual bones with tweezers. (You will have 2 fillets.) Slice the salmon into 4 pieces, cutting two from each fillet. Set aside in a cool place.

2 For the stuffing, thinly slice the leeks, courgette and carrots on the diagonal. Steam the vegetables until just tender, allowing approximately 6 minutes for the carrots, 4 minutes for leeks and 2 minutes for the courgette. Leave to cool slightly.

3 Divide the steamed vegetables between the salmon fillets, placing them at the end of one short side. Season with salt and pepper, then roll the fillet to enclose the vegetables. Place the rolled fish parcels on a large sheet of lightly greased foil. Bring the sides of the foil together and seal tightly. Set aside.

4 To make the beurre blanc, place the shallots in a heavy-based pan and add the vinegar, white wine and half the lime juice. Cover and simmer over a low heat until almost all of the liquid has evaporated, about 15-20 minutes.

5 Meanwhile blanch the lime zest in boiling water for about 4 minutes. Allow to cool, then chop finely.

6 Remove the shallots from the heat and allow to cool slightly, then whisk in the cream. Gradually whisk in the butter, one piece at a time, ensuring each piece is incorporated before adding the next. Once all of the butter is incorporated, add the chopped lime zest and ground coriander. Season with salt and pepper to taste, adding a little more lime juice if necessary. Cover and keep warm.

7 Place the foil-wrapped salmon parcels in a preheated oven at 200°C (400°F) mark 6 and cook for 10-12 minutes until the salmon is just opaque. Carefully place each salmon parcel on a warmed serving plate and add a generous swirl of sauce. Serve at once, with Potato and Courgette Soufflés (see page 101).

Pan-fried John Dory with Wild Mushrooms and Chinese 'Seaweed'

900 g (2 lb) spring greens, washed and
  stalks removed
4 shallots
30 ml (2 tbsp) olive oil
350 ml (12 fl oz) good quality fish stock
350 ml (12 fl oz) fruity red wine
  (eg Grenache or Gamay)
4 thyme sprigs, leaves only
5-10 ml (1-2 tsp) balsamic vinegar
40 g (1½ oz) unsalted butter
400 g (14 oz) wild mushrooms (eg hedgehog
  fungus, chanterelles), cleaned and sliced
salt and freshly ground black pepper
groundnut oil for deep-frying
a little caster sugar
4 John Dory fillets, each about 200 g (7 oz)
seasoned flour, for dusting
knob of clarified butter
squeeze of lemon juice

1 Roll up each spring green leaf tightly into a cylinder and slice across the roll, as finely as possible, to yield long, fine strands. Dry thoroughly.

2 Finely dice 2 shallots; chop the others.

3 Heat 15 ml (1 tbsp) olive oil in a pan, add the finely diced shallots and cook until softened. Add the fish stock, wine, thyme and balsamic vinegar. Bring to the boil and simmer to reduce to about one third of the original volume. Strain through a fine sieve into a clean pan; keep warm.

4 Heat half of the butter with the remaining oil in a frying pan. Add the chopped shallots and sauté until softened. Add the sliced mushrooms and seasoning. Sauté over a high heat for 6-7 minutes until tender. Set aside; keep warm.

5 Heat the groundnut oil in a deep-fat fryer to 190°C (375°F) and deep-fry the greens in batches until they change colour. Remove and drain thoroughly on kitchen paper. Season liberally with salt and pepper and sprinkle with sugar. Keep warm.

6 Dust the John Dory fillets lightly with seasoned flour. Heat a large frying pan until fairly hot, then add a knob of clarified butter. Add the fish, flesh-side down, and cook for 1-1½ minutes, then turn and cook on the other side for 1-1½ minutes.

7 Meanwhile, return the sauce to the heat and whisk in the remaining 20 g (¾ oz) butter, a piece at a time, until the sauce is glossy.

8 Squeeze a little lemon juice over the mushrooms and pile into the centre of the warmed serving plates. Place the fish on top and arrange a mound of 'Chinese seaweed' alongside. Flood the plates with the red wine sauce and serve immediately.

Poultry
& Game

Poached Chicken 'Hindle Wakes' with Lemon Sauce and Forcemeat Balls

This dish is based on a traditional festive dish from Lancashire. The contrast of black pudding and white chicken flesh strikes a medieval note, and the name may be derived from the Old English 'Hen de la Wake'.

2 large, free-range chicken breasts, each
    about 225 g (8 oz)
600 ml (1 pint) well-flavoured reduced
    chicken stock

Stuffing:
1 black pudding, about 175 g (6 oz),
    skinned and coarsely chopped
125 g (4 oz) 'no soak' prunes, roughly
    chopped
50 g (2 oz) blanched almonds
salt and freshly ground black pepper

Forcemeat Balls:
125 g (4 oz) thick-cut, smoked streaky
    bacon, derinded and diced
1 celery stick, diced
175 g (6 oz) fatty pork, coarsely minced
50 g (2 oz) fresh breadcrumbs
2.5 ml (½ tsp) ground mace
15-30 ml (1-2 tbsp) finely chopped parsley
freshly ground black pepper
flour, for coating
1 egg, beaten
125 g (4 oz) dried breadcrumbs
oil for deep-frying

Lemon Sauce:
300 ml (½ pint) well-flavoured reduced
    chicken stock
grated rind and juice of 1 lemon
110 g (4 oz) unsalted butter, diced
10 ml (2 tsp) plain flour

1 To prepare the stuffing, heat a non-stick frying pan, then add the black pudding and prunes. Fry until the pudding changes colour and the mixture is slightly amalgamated. Add the almonds and season liberally with salt and pepper. Allow to cool.

2 To make the forcemeat balls, combine the bacon, celery, minced pork, fresh breadcrumbs, mace and parsley together in a bowl. Season well with pepper (the bacon should provide sufficient salt). Mix the ingredients together thoroughly. Form the mixture into 12 walnut-sized balls.

3 Using a sharp knife, cut a deep pocket in the side of each chicken breast. Mould the black pudding stuffing into two plump cylinders, using your hands, then use to fill the chicken breasts. Secure with wooden toothpicks or bamboo skewers.

4 Heat the stock in a shallow pan, add the stuffed chicken breasts and poach very gently for 20-30 minutes until tender.

5 In the meantime, cook the forcemeat balls. Roll each one in seasoned flour, dip in beaten egg, then coat in dry breadcrumbs. Heat the oil for deep-frying in a deep-fat fryer until a piece of bread dropped in will turn golden in 1 minute. Add the forcemeat balls and deep-fry for 4-5 minutes until golden brown. Remove and drain on kitchen paper; keep hot.

6 Meanwhile, make the sauce. Put the stock in a saucepan with the lemon rind and juice. Bring to the boil and boil to reduce by half. Blend the flour with 10 ml (2 tsp) of the butter to make a beurre manié. Whisk the remaining butter into the sauce, a piece at a time. Finally whisk in the beurre manié and cook until the sauce thickens without boiling.

7 Remove the toothpicks or skewers from the chicken and carve each breast into 6 thick slices. Arrange 3 slices on each warmed serving plate. Spoon over the lemon sauce and serve, accompanied by the forcemeat balls and Spinach and Cucumber Ribbons (see page 88).

Roasted Chicken with Wild Mushrooms, and Potato and Celeriac Mash

2 free-range chickens, each about 1.4 kg (3 lb) in weight

Stuffing:
80 g (3 oz) flat-leaf parsley, stalks removed, finely chopped
40 g (1½ oz) fresh breadcrumbs
40 g (1½ oz) unsalted butter, at room temperature
salt and freshly ground black pepper

Jus:
600 ml (1 pint) good chicken stock
few thyme sprigs

Mushrooms:
30 ml (2 tbsp) olive oil
400 g (14 oz) wild mushrooms (eg hedgehog fungus or chanterelles), cleaned and sliced

Potato and Celeriac Mash:
600 g (1 lb 2 oz) waxy potatoes, (such as Charlotte)
300 g (10 oz) celeriac
50 g (2 oz) unsalted butter
50 g (2 oz) Parmesan cheese, freshly grated

1 Carefully remove the legs and wings from the chickens (see note), making sure that the skin over the breasts is not broken. (You may also prefer to remove the wishbone at this point to make carving easier.)

2 To prepare the stuffing, in a bowl mix together the parsley, breadcrumbs, butter and seasoning.

3 Put the stuffing into a piping bag fitted with a plain nozzle and pipe the stuffing mixture between the skin and the breast meat. Smooth the stuffing evenly under the skin. Season the chicken breasts with salt and pepper. Place in a roasting tin and roast in a preheated oven at 200°C (400°F) mark 6 for 25 minutes.

4 Meanwhile, peel the potatoes and celeriac and cut into even-sized chunks. Cook in salted water to cover until tender. Drain well, then mash smoothly. Beat in the unsalted butter and Parmesan. Season with salt and pepper to taste; keep warm.

5 In the meantime pour the chicken stock into a small saucepan, bring to the boil and reduce by half to concentrate the flavour. Take off the heat, add a few thyme sprigs and set aside to infuse for 15 minutes. Check the seasoning and keep warm.

6 Remove the chicken from the oven and leave to rest in a warm place for 15 minutes. Heat the olive oil in a frying pan, add the wild mushrooms and sauté over a high heat for 6-7 minutes until tender.

7 To serve, remove the chicken breasts from the bone. Spoon some mash onto each warmed serving plate, place a chicken breast on top and scatter the mushrooms around. Pour over the jus and serve at once.

Note: Use the chicken legs and wings as the basis for the stock.

Chicken Sauté in Ginger Sauce with Japanese Mushroom Fritters

4 chicken breast fillets
10 g (⅓ oz) fresh root ginger, peeled and
  grated
150 ml (¼ pint) soy sauce
75 ml (5 tbsp) saké (Japanese rice wine)
15 ml (1 tbsp) vegetable oil
10 g (⅓ oz) butter
15 ml (1 tbsp) cornflour, blended with
  30 ml (2 tbsp) water

Japanese Mushroom Fritters:
100 g (3½ oz) flour
pinch of salt
150 ml (¼ pint) lukewarm water
  (approximately)
2 egg whites
200 g (7 oz) Japanese mushrooms (eg
  shiitake, maitake)
corn oil for deep-frying

1 Put the chicken fillets in a shallow non-reactive dish with the grated ginger, soy sauce and saké. Turn to coat with the mixture and leave to marinate for about 15 minutes.

2 Meanwhile, make the mushroom fritter batter. Sift the flour and salt into a bowl, then gradually mix in the water to form a smooth, thick batter. In a separate bowl, whisk the egg whites until stiff, then fold into the batter.

3 Remove the chicken from the marinade, reserving the marinade. Heat the oil in a frying pan and add the butter. When melted together, add the chicken and fry over a high heat for about 1 minute. Reduce the heat to moderate and fry for 5 minutes on each side until tender.

4 Meanwhile cook the mushroom fritters. Heat the oil for deep-frying in a deep saucepan or deep-fat fryer to 190°C (375°F). When it is hot, cook the mushrooms in batches. Dip them into the batter, one at a time, then immerse in the hot oil. When the mushroom fritters rise to the surface, remove with a slotted spoon and drain well on kitchen paper; keep hot.

5 Transfer the chicken to a warmed dish; keep warm. Strain the reserved marinade into the pan and boil to reduce for about 3 minutes. Add the blended cornflour and cook, stirring, for 1 minute.

6 Pour the sauce over the chicken and arrange the mushroom fritters alongside. Serve accompanied by Parsley Rice (see page 108) and Three-colour Vegetable Stir-fry (see page 90).

Guinea Fowl Breasts with Calvados, Apple and Onion Sauce

60 ml (4 tbsp) olive oil
1 onion, halved and thinly sliced
1 cox's apple
45 ml (3 tbsp) Calvados
300 ml (½ pint) homemade chicken stock
4 guinea fowl breasts, with skin
30-45 ml (2-3 tbsp) double cream
  (optional)
salt and freshly ground black pepper

To Garnish:
1 cox's apple
15 g (½ oz) unsalted butter
7.5 ml (1½ tsp) brown sugar

1 Heat 30 ml (2 tbsp) of the oil in a heavy-based frying pan. Add the onion and fry gently until softened and starting to brown.

2 Meanwhile, peel, core and slice the apple. Add to the onions and fry over a low heat until softened and beginning to brown. Increase the heat, add the Calvados and bubble to reduce. Add the chicken stock, a little at a time, continuing to reduce the sauce to a fairly thick consistency. Transfer to a blender or food processor and work to a purée, then pass through a sieve into a clean pan.

3 In the meantime, heat the remaining oil in the frying pan. Add the guinea fowl breasts, skin-side down, and fry quickly over a high heat until the skin is golden brown. Turn the breasts over in the pan and immediately remove from the heat. Transfer the guinea fowl to a roasting tin, skin-side up, and cook in a preheated oven at 180°C (350°F) mark 4 for about 10 minutes until tender.

4 Meanwhile, prepare the garnish. Peel the apple and slice horizontally into rings. Remove the core from each slice with a small pastry cutter. Melt the unsalted butter in a pan. Add the apple rings, sprinkle with the brown sugar and cook over a high heat until caramelised.

5 Reheat the sauce, stir in the cream (if using) and season with salt and pepper to taste.

6 To serve, spoon the sauce onto warmed serving plates and place the guinea fowl on top. Garnish with the caramelised apple slices and serve at once, with Broccoli Timbales (see page 89) and Butternut Squash Balls (see page 98).

Breast of Gressingham Duck Wildfowler-style

2 oven-ready Gressingham ducks
salt and freshly ground black pepper

Sauce:
reserved duck bones
1 carrot, chopped
1 onion, chopped
1 celery stick, chopped
dash of Madeira
10 ml (2 tsp) chopped tarragon
1.5 litres (2½ pints) duck or chicken stock

Stuffing:
25 g (1 oz) rindless streaky bacon, minced
25 g (1 oz) butter
50 g (2 oz) button mushrooms, minced
50 g (2 oz) morels, minced
2.5 ml (½ tsp) crushed garlic
½ bay leaf
4 sage leaves
1 thyme sprig
25 ml (1 fl oz) Madeira
1 egg white
120 ml (4 fl oz) double cream

1 Take the legs from the ducks and remove the meat from the bones, trimming away any tendons and fat and reserving the bones for the sauce. Dice the leg meat and set aside in the refrigerator. Remove the outer wing joints, leaving the inner part attached to the breast; leave the breast on the bone.

2 To make the sauce, put the duck bones in a deep heavy-based pan with the chopped vegetables and brown over a moderate heat. Deglaze the pan with the Madeira, then add the chopped tarragon. Cover with stock. Bring to the boil, skim the surface, then simmer for 1-2 hours. Strain through a fine sieve and return to the pan. Reduce by about half until the sauce is shiny and a deep mahogany colour.

3 Meanwhile, prepare the stuffing. Put the minced bacon in a heavy-based pan over a medium heat until the fat starts to run. Add the butter and melt, then add the mushrooms and morels and sauté for 3-4 minutes. Add the garlic and sauté for a further 3 minutes. Add the herbs and Madeira, then simmer over a medium heat until the liquid is evaporated and the mixture is almost dry. Discard the herbs and allow to cool.

4 Put the chilled duck leg meat in a food processor and process until smooth. With the motor running, add the egg white through the feeder tube and process for 20-30 seconds. Scrape down the side of the bowl, then add the cream and process briefly until evenly incorporated. Transfer to a bowl and fold in the cooled mushroom mixture.

5 Transfer the mixture to a piping bag fitted with the plain nozzle. Loosen the skin on the duck breasts and pipe a quarter of the mixture under the skin of each duck breast. Leave in refrigerator until needed.

6 Season the duck breasts with salt and pepper and bake in a preheated oven at 180°C (350°F) mark 4 for 25 minutes until just cooked. Leave to rest in a warm place for 5-10 minutes. Reheat the sauce.

7 To serve remove the whole breasts from the duck carcasses and slice each one into 4 or 5 pieces. Fan out on warmed serving plates and surround with the sauce. Serve with Potato Galettes (see page 106), a creamed purée of leeks, and steamed and sautéed carrots, parsnips and celeriac.

Breast of Duck with Prune and Pistachio Stuffing

For the stuffing, you will need to soak the prunes and pistachio nuts in the Madeira overnight.

150 g (5 oz) dried prunes
20 g (¾ oz) pistachio nuts
100 ml (3½ fl oz) Madeira
4 duck breast fillets
30 ml (2 tbsp) thin honey
2 cloves garlic, chopped
15 ml (1 tbsp) olive oil
200 ml (⅓ pint) lamb stock
25 ml (5 tsp) double cream
salt and freshly ground pepper

1 Put the dried prunes and pistachio nuts in a small bowl, pour on the Madeira and leave to soak overnight.

2 The next day, drain the prunes and nuts, reserving the marinade.

3 Prick the skin of each duck breast in several places, then turn the duck breasts over and make horizontal cuts, three-quarters of the way through the meat, so that the duck breasts open out flat.

4 Arrange a line of prunes down the centre of two of the fillets. Sprinkle with pistachio nuts, then cover with the other fillets; reserve the remaining prunes and nuts (approximately one third) for the sauce. Tie the fillets together securing with string at 1 cm (½ inch) intervals.

5 Smear the honey and garlic over the joints and place in a shallow dish. Pour on the reserved marinade and leave for 1 hour.

6 Remove the duck breast joints from the marinade with a slotted spoon; reserve the marinade for the sauce.

7 Heat the oil in a frying pan. Season the duck breast joints with salt and pepper, add to the hot oil and sear over a high heat, turning the joints until the skin is golden brown all over.

8 Transfer the joints to a roasting tin and cover with foil. Cook near the bottom of a preheated oven at 190°C (375°F) mark 5 for 40 minutes.

9 Meanwhile to make the sauce, bring the lamb stock to the boil in a pan. Add the remaining prunes and pistachio nuts, with the reserved marinade. Boil to reduce for 10 minutes. Transfer to a blender or food processor and work until smooth. Pass through a fine sieve into a clean pan. Heat through over a medium heat, add the cream and season with salt and pepper to taste. If necessary, sieve the sauce again before using.

10 To serve, slice the duck breasts, remove the string and arrange on warmed serving plates. Pour the sauce around one side of the meat and serve at once, with Potato and Wild Mushroom Cake (see page 102), and Tiered Shredded Vegetable Crowns (see page 95).

Pan-fried Breast of Wild Cotswold Mallard with a Port Sauce, Redcurrant Sauce, Wild Mushrooms and Caramelised Shallots

Properly hung mallard has a wonderful gamey taste and is perfect for this recipe. If unobtainable use Gressingham ducks instead (see note).

2 mallards
salt and freshly ground black pepper

Stock:
reserved duck carcasses
knob of butter
2 medium onions, roughly chopped
2 large carrots, roughly chopped
10 juniper berries, crushed
salt
12 peppercorns
175 g (6 oz) flat mushrooms, chopped

Marinade and Port Sauce:
300 ml (½ pint) port
30 ml (2 tbsp) thin honey
600 ml (1 pint) reduced duck stock (see method)
knob of butter

Redcurrant Sauce:
50 g (2 oz) redcurrants
5-10 ml (1-2 tsp) granulated sugar

For Cooking:
butter and olive oil

To Assemble:
125 g (4 oz) shallots, peeled
50 g (2 oz) wild mushrooms (preferably fresh yellow chanterelles), cleaned and trimmed
1 clove garlic, crushed

To Garnish:
thyme and rosemary sprigs
oil for deep-frying

1 A day ahead, remove the breasts and legs from the ducks and refrigerate. For the stock, cut up the carcasses and brown in a preheated oven at 230°C (450°F) mark 8 for 10 minutes. Heat the butter in a large saucepan, add the onions and carrots, and fry gently until softened. Add the carcasses, juniper berries, a little salt, the peppercorns and chopped mushrooms. Add sufficient boiling water to cover. Bring to a gentle simmer and skim off any froth from the surface. Cover and simmer for 3 hours, topping up with water as necessary. Strain through a fine sieve into a clean pan, pressing out as much juice as possible from the ingredients. Bring to the boil and reduce to 600 ml (1 pint). Cool and refrigerate overnight.

2 The next day, remove the fat which will have solidified on the surface of the stock.

3 For the marinade, combine 120 ml (4 fl oz) of the port with the honey in a shallow dish (large enough to hold the duck breasts in a single layer). Add the duck breasts, ensuring the skin is uppermost and not in the marinade. Leave to marinate for 1½ hours.

4 Meanwhile, prepare the redcurrant sauce. Put the redcurrants in a heavy-based pan with the sugar. Heat gently until the sugar is dissolved, then cook until reduced and thickened. Strain through a nylon sieve into a bowl and set aside.

5 Remove the duck breasts from the marinade and pat dry, reserving marinade. Finely score the skin lengthwise and season with salt and pepper. Set aside.

6 Cut the ankles off the duck legs and extract the tendons. Season the duck legs, smear with a little butter and roast in a preheated oven at 200°C (400°F) mark 6 for 20 minutes.

7 Remove the outer layer from the shallots, and divide into single segments. Heat a knob of butter in a small heavy-based pan, add the shallots and fry, turning occasionally, for 20 minutes, or until soft and golden.

8 To make the port sauce, add the marinade to the duck stock and reduce over a moderate heat until it starts to thicken. At the same time, reduce 175 ml (6 fl oz) port in another pan until it starts to thicken. Pour the reduced stock through a fine sieve into the port and reduce further until the sauce starts to bubble. Remove from the heat and check the seasoning. Beat in a knob of butter, a little at a time, to glaze.

9 Preheat a heavy-based frying pan over a high heat. Add a knob of butter and a little olive oil. When the butter has melted, add the duck breasts, skin-side down, sear quickly, then lower the heat to moderate and fry for 3 minutes. Turn and cook the other side for 3 minutes. Meanwhile, put the duck legs on a grill rack under a very hot grill for about 2 minutes until crisp. Wrap the duck breasts individually in foil and leave to rest in a warm place while preparing the mushrooms and garnish.

10 Heat a knob of butter in a pan, add the mushrooms with the garlic and a little salt, and fry over a low heat for 2 minutes. Meanwhile, for the garnish, heat the oil for deep-frying and deep-fry the sprigs of thyme and rosemary in the hot oil until they start to curl; remove and dry on kitchen paper.

11 To serve, slice each duck breast thinly and arrange overlapping on each warmed serving plate, with the duck leg on top. Spoon some of the port sauce around the duck breast, dot with the redcurrant sauce and feather with a skewer. Garnish with the sautéed wild mushrooms, caramelised shallots and deep-fried herbs. Serve with Spinach Purée with Pine Nuts (see page 90) and Creamed Potatoes with Truffle (see page 105).

Note: If using Gressingham duck, flash fry, skin-side down, in a very hot, dry pan to break down the fat; once some fat has been rendered, the temperature can be reduced. You will also need to allow a slightly longer cooking time, as the breast will be thicker than on a mallard.

A young bird, shot early in the season and with no membrane under the skin, should not be scored. Avoid birds which have been shot through the breast.

Medallion of Ostrich stuffed with Scallops, served with a Tortellini of Turnip Tops and a Cardamom and Vanilla Sauce

Ostrich is becoming increasingly popular. It is a very lean, tender meat with a flavour somewhat reminiscent of sirloin steak.

450 g (1 lb) ostrich fillet
8 large scallops, cleaned
oil, for brushing
salt and freshly ground black pepper

Pasta Dough:
110 g (4 oz) plain flour
1 egg (size 3)
15 ml (1 tbsp) water
7.5-10 ml (1½-2 tsp) paprika

Pasta Filling:
knob of butter
50 g (2 oz) onion, finely diced
110 g (4 oz) turnip top leaves, roughly chopped
5 ml (1 tsp) black sesame seeds
salt and freshly ground black pepper

Cardamom and Vanilla Sauce:
½ vanilla pod
4 cardamom pods
300 ml (½ pint) chicken stock
150 ml (¼ pint) whipping cream

1 First make the pasta dough. Put all of the ingredients into a food processor and process until the dough binds together to form a ball. Wrap in cling film and leave to rest while you prepare the filling.

2 To make the filling, heat the butter in a pan, add the onion and fry until softened, then add the turnip tops and cook for 1-2 minutes until just wilted. Transfer to a chopping board and chop very finely. Return the turnip tops to the frying pan, add the sesame seeds and cook for about 2 minutes. Season generously with salt and pepper. Transfer to a cold dish and allow to cool.

3 Roll out the pasta using a pasta machine, passing the dough through repeatedly and narrowing the setting by one notch each time until you reach the thinnest setting.

4 Lay the resulting strip of pasta on a clean surface and brush lightly with a little water. Cut out rounds using a 7.5-10 cm (3-4 inch) plain cutter. Place 5 ml (1 tsp) of the turnip top mixture in the centre of each round and fold in half, pressing the edges of the pasta together to seal. Take the resulting crescent shape and wrap around your index finger nipping the two ends of the crescent together. Set aside on a plate until ready to cook.

5 To make the sauce, extract the seeds from the vanilla pod and set aside. Crush the vanilla pod and whole cardamoms together, using a pestle and mortar or spice grinder. Heat the chicken stock in a pan, then add the cream, vanilla seeds, ground cardamoms and vanilla pod. Reduce by about half until the sauce is slightly thickened and has a good flavour. Strain through a sieve into a clean pan; keep warm.

6 Cut the ostrich fillet into 4 medallions. Preheat a metal skewer over a flame or hot plate until red hot. Sear the scallops on one side, with the hot skewer to make a criss-cross pattern. Preheat a griddle or heavy-based frying pan and oil the pan. Add the ostrich medallions and cook for 3-4 minutes on each side; they should still be pink in the middle. A few minutes before the ostrich will be cooked, add the scallops and cook for 1-2 minutes each side until light golden in colour.

7 Meanwhile, cook the pasta in a large pan of boiling salted water for about 3-4 minutes until *al dente*, tender but firm to the bite. Drain thoroughly.

8 When the ostrich is cooked to your liking make a horizontal slit in each one to form a pocket. Pop 2 scallops into each pocket, pattern-side up.

9 To serve, place the stuffed ostrich medallions on warmed serving plates with the tortellini pasta. Serve with glazed turnips and steamed vegetables. Flood the plates with the cardamom and vanilla sauce and serve immediately.

Pan-fried Duck on a Port and Wine Sauce

4 duck breast fillets
salt and freshly ground black pepper

Sauce:
60 ml (4 tbsp) vegetable oil
2 shallots, roughly chopped
1 celery stick, roughly chopped
1 carrot, roughly chopped
30 g (1¼ oz) brown sugar
100 ml (3½ fl oz) port
200 ml (⅓ pint) red wine
300 ml (½ pint) chicken stock
50 g (2 oz) unsalted butter, diced

1 To make the sauce, heat the oil in a pan, add the shallots, celery and carrot and fry until well browned. Add the sugar and cook until lightly caramelised. Add the port and wine and reduce to about 100 ml (3½ fl oz). Add the stock and reduce until the sauce is thick enough to lightly coat the back of a wooden spoon. Pass through a sieve into a clean pan and gradually whisk in the butter a piece at a time, over a low heat.

2 Place a heavy-based frying pan over a high heat. Season the duck breasts, add to the pan, skin-side down, and sear for 2 minutes. Turn the duck breasts over and sear the other side for 2 minutes. Transfer to a roasting tin and cook in a preheated oven at 190°C (375°F) mark 5 for 8-12 minutes, or longer if preferred, according to taste and the size of the duck breasts; they should still be pink in the centre. Leave to rest in a warm place before carving.

3 To serve, slice the duck and arrange on warmed serving plates. Pour on the sauce and serve with Potatoes Lyonnaise (see page 103), Braised Cabbage Rolls (see page 92) and Root Vegetable Purée (see page 98).

Stuffed Pigeon Breast with a Lattice Puff Pastry Crust served with an Elderberry Sauce

150 g (5 oz) ready-made puff pastry
4 pigeon breasts
4 slices Prosciutto (or Parma ham)
1 egg yolk, beaten

Stuffing:
15 g (½ oz) unsalted butter
1 shallot, finely diced
70 g (2½ oz) open cap mushrooms, finely chopped
salt and freshly ground black pepper
pinch of freshly grated nutmeg

Elderberry Sauce:
400 ml (14 fl oz) pigeon stock
20 g (¾ oz) unsalted butter
20 g (¾ oz) plain flour
100 ml (3½ fl oz) elderberry juice
a little sugar, to taste

1 To prepare the stuffing, melt the butter in a frying pan, add the shallot and cook until soft. Add the mushrooms and increase the heat. Continue to cook until all the liquid from the mushrooms has evaporated and you are left with a paste. Season with salt, pepper and nutmeg to taste. Leave to cool.

2 To make the elderberry sauce, put the pigeon stock in a saucepan and boil to reduce by approximately two thirds. In a separate pan, heat the butter until melted, then stir in the flour. Cook for 1 minute, then gradually stir in the reduced pigeon stock and elderberry juice. Season with salt and pepper and add a little sugar to taste; keep warm.

3 Roll out the puff pastry to a 3 mm (⅛ inch) thickness and cut four rectangles, about 15 x 10 cm (6 x 4 inches). Roll with a pastry lattice roller (see note).

4 Cut a deep, horizontal slit in each pigeon breast to make a pocket. Fill each pocket with the mushroom stuffing. Wrap each pigeon breast in a slice of prosciutto, then carefully envelope in a pastry lattice. Brush with egg yolk to glaze and place on a baking tray. Cook in a preheated oven at 220°C (425°F) mark 7 for about 7-8 minutes until the pastry is golden brown.

5 To serve, carefully transfer each pigeon breast to a warmed serving plate and surround with the sauce. Serve with Puréed Parsnip Timbales (see page 99) and Lemon-glazed Carrot Ribbons (see page 94).

Note: A pastry lattice roller is a plastic or perspex cylinder with inset 'blades'. As the lattice roller moves over the pastry it cuts slits and, when the pastry is lifted from the surface, these slits open up to form the lattice. You can obtain lattice rollers from good kitchen shops and mail order cookware suppliers.

Pot-roasted Venison in Fig Wine with Mushrooms

For this recipe, you will need to prepare the fig wine (see below) at least 1 month ahead. If possible, marinate the venison in the fig wine overnight before cooking.

4 venison fillets, each about 150 g (5 oz)
4 shallots, finely chopped
1 bunch of thyme sprigs
1 clove garlic, crushed
450 ml (¾ pint) fig wine (see below)
plain flour, for dusting
salt and freshly ground black pepper
30 ml (2 tbsp) olive oil
225 g (8 oz) mushrooms, roughly chopped

To Garnish:
4 fresh figs, quartered

1 If possible marinate the venison overnight or for at least 6 hours before cooking. Place the venison steaks in a shallow dish and sprinkle with the shallots, thyme and garlic. Pour on the fig wine and leave to marinate for at least 6 hours.

2 Remove the venison steaks from the marinade and pat dry. Reserve the marinade. Season the flour with salt and pepper and use to dust the venison steaks.

3 Heat the oil in a flameproof casserole and brown the venison steaks, two at a time, on both sides over a high heat. Remove and set aside.

4 Add the chopped mushrooms to the casserole and fry until softened. Return the venison to the casserole and pour in the reserved marinade. Bring to the boil, then lower the heat and cook gently for approximately 1½ hours.

5 Remove the venison from the casserole and place in a warmed dish; keep warm. Discard the thyme and reduce the sauce slightly until rich and shiny.

6 To serve, spoon the mushrooms into a mound in the middle of each serving plate and position the venison on top. Pour over the reduced sauce and garnish with the fresh figs. Serve with Spicy Red Cabbage with Apple (see page 91), Parmesan Puff Potatoes (see page 104) and French beans.

Fig Wine: Place 500 g (1 lb 2 oz) dried figs in a large saucepan and add cold water to cover. Slowly bring to the boil, lower the heat and simmer for 5 minutes. Drain and rinse with cold water.

Return the figs to the pan and add 1 bay leaf; 15 ml (1 tbsp) coriander seeds; 1 cinnamon stick; 2 green cardamom pods, lightly crushed; ½ orange, sliced; 200 ml (⅓ pint) Madeira and 2 litres (3½ pints) red wine. Bring to the boil and simmer for 10 minutes. Remove from the heat and leave to cool *completely.*

Add 100 ml (3½ fl oz) brandy. Pour the fig wine into sterilised jars and seal tightly. Leave for 1 month and strain before using.

Saddle of Roe Deer in a Port Sauce

600 g (1 lb 5 oz), filleted saddle of roe deer
  venison, trimmed
salt and freshly ground black pepper
35 g (1¼ oz) clarified butter
250 ml (8 fl oz) port
2 shallots, chopped
500 ml (16 fl oz) veal stock
1 thyme sprig
30 g (1 oz) unsalted butter, chilled and
  diced
flat-leaf parsley, to garnish

1 Cut the venison into 4 even portions and season with salt and pepper. Heat the clarified butter in a heavy-based frying pan and quickly sear the venison over a high heat for about 2 minutes, turning to seal on all sides. Remove the meat from the pan and transfer to a wire rack; leave to rest.

2 Pour off excess butter from the pan, then deglaze with the port and add the shallots. Reduce over a high heat by about half, then add the veal stock and thyme and reduce again by half. Pass the sauce through a fine sieve into a clean pan; keep warm.

3 Before serving, reheat the venison in a preheated oven at 200°C (400°F) mark 6 for about 10 minutes. Meanwhile, whisk the butter into the sauce, a piece at a time, over a low heat. Check the seasoning.

4 Remove the venison from the oven and cut each portion into 5 slices. Arrange on warmed serving plates with a mound of Buttered Spinach with Nutmeg (see page 90). Spoon the sauce around the meat and garnish with parsley. Serve at once, with Parsley Potatoes (see page 101).

Meat
Dishes

Fillet of Aberdeen Angus Beef Roasted in a Salt Crust infused with Herbs

Salt Crust:
450 g (1 lb) sea salt
25 g (1 oz) thyme leaves
3 rosemary sprigs, leaves only
2 egg whites
150 ml (¼ pint) water
300 g (10 oz) plain flour

For the Beef:
800 g (1 lb 12 oz) whole fillet of Aberdeen Angus beef
15 ml (1 tbsp) butter
15 ml (1 tbsp) olive oil
15 ml (1 tbsp) fresh thyme leaves

To Glaze:
beaten egg yolk
rock salt

Red Wine Sauce:
15 g (½ oz) dried trompette de mort (or porcini) mushrooms
450 ml (¾ pint) well-flavoured red wine beef stock
60 ml (2 fl oz) Madeira (preferably Malmsey)
25 g (1 oz) butter, in pieces
salt and freshly ground black pepper

1 Prepare the salt crust at least 3-4 hours in advance if possible, but no longer than 24 hours ahead. Place the salt and herbs in a food processor and process until the herbs are finely chopped. Add the egg whites and water and work until evenly mixed. Add the flour and process until a smooth dough is formed. Transfer to a bowl, cover with cling film and leave to rest at room temperature for several hours or overnight if possible. (A longer resting time allows more time for the flavour of the herbs to infuse into the crust.)

2 Soak the dried mushrooms for the sauce in warm water to cover for 30 minutes.

3 To prepare the beef, pat dry with kitchen paper and heat the butter and oil together in a heavy-based frying pan. Add the beef and sear on all sides over a high heat. Transfer to a plate to rest for 5-10 minutes.

4 Meanwhile, roll out the salt crust dough to a rectangle, large enough to wrap around the beef. Sprinkle the beef with the thyme leaves and wrap in the herb crust, sealing the edges well. Brush the dough with beaten egg yolk and sprinkle with rock salt to glaze. Lift onto a baking sheet.

5 Cook in a preheated oven at 180°C (350°F) mark 4 for 30 minutes for rare beef, or slightly longer for medium rare. Remove from the oven and leave to rest in a warm place for 40-50 minutes to allow the beef to absorb the flavours of the herbs and salt crust.

6 Meanwhile, make the sauce. Drain the mushrooms, straining and reserving half of the liquid. Bring the stock to the boil in a saucepan, add the mushrooms and reserved liquor with the Madeira. Reduce until the sauce is thickened. Just before serving whisk in the butter, a piece at a time. Season with salt and pepper to taste.

7 To serve, cut around the edges of the salt crust and lift the top away. Take out the beef and discard the salt crust. Carve the meat into slices and arrange on warmed serving plates. Serve with the rich red wine sauce, Caramelised Shallots and Garlic (see page 96), Horseradish Potatoes (see page 104) and Glazed Radishes (see page 98).

Angus Steak with Whisky and Green Peppercorn Sauce

4 Angus beef fillet steaks, each about
175-225 g (6 -8 oz)
a little olive oil
1 clove garlic, crushed
15 ml (1 tbsp) crushed black peppercorns

Green Peppercorn Sauce:
knob of butter
3 shallots, finely chopped
200 ml (7 fl oz) light beef or chicken stock
10 ml (2 tsp) Dijon mustard
10 ml (2 tsp) Worcestershire sauce
2-3 parsley sprigs
10 ml (2 tsp) green peppercorns in brine,
* drained*
125 ml (4 fl oz) double cream or crème
* fraîche*
15-30 ml (1-2 tbsp) whisky
salt and freshly ground black pepper

1 Rub the steaks all over with a little olive oil, the garlic and crushed black peppercorns. Set aside in a cool place.

2 To make the sauce, melt the butter in a pan, add the shallots, cover and sweat until softened. Add the stock and simmer until reduced by about half. Add the mustard, Worcestershire sauce and parsley. Transfer to a blender or food processor and work until smooth. Return the mixture to the pan and add the green peppercorns. Cook for 2-3 minutes; cover and set aside.

3 To cook the steaks, oil a cast-iron grill plate and heat to sizzling. Place the steaks on the grill plate and cook for 4-5 minutes each side according to taste, turning regularly and brushing with extra oil if they start to stick to the pan. Set aside to rest in a warm place whilst finishing the sauce.

4 Reheat the sauce, then add the cream and whisky. Cook gently for 2-3 minutes. Check the seasoning.

5 Slice each steak and fan out on warmed serving plates. Spoon over the sauce and serve immediately, accompanied by Mejadarra with Mushrooms (see page 107) and Beetroot and Preserved Lime Salad (see page 97).

Note: If you do not have a grill pan, cook the steaks in a heavy-based frying pan or under a preheated grill, basting frequently with oil.

Roast Fillet of Scotch Beef on a Rich Red Wine Sauce

4 Angus beef fillet steaks, each about
  125-175 g (4 -6 oz)
50 g (2 oz) unsalted butter

Sauce:
50 g (2 oz) butter
15 ml (1 tbsp) olive oil
4 shallots, chopped
1 large carrot, chopped
2 celery sticks, chopped
1 clove garlic, chopped
1 bay leaf
1 bottle red wine
1.2 litres (2 pints) beef or veal stock
salt and freshly ground black pepper

1 First make the sauce. Melt half of the butter with the olive oil in a saucepan. Add the vegetables and garlic and sweat over a medium heat for about 10 minutes until softened. Add the bay leaf and red wine. Boil to reduce until the sauce is a syrupy consistency.

2 Add the stock and simmer for approximately 20 minutes, scraping down the sides of the pan frequently.

3 Pass the sauce through a sieve into a small saucepan. Reduce the sauce until it is thick enough to thinly coat the back of a spoon. Whisk in the remaining butter, a knob at a time, over a medium heat. Check the seasoning. Transfer the sauce to a warmed jug and keep warm over a pan of hot water.

4 To cook the beef, heat the unsalted butter in a sauté pan. Add the fillet steaks and quickly seal on all sides. Transfer to a shallow roasting tin. Cook in a preheated oven at 220°C (425°F) mark 7 for 4-6 minutes, according to taste.

5 Cut each fillet steak into 4 slices and place on warmed serving plates. Pour a little of the red wine sauce around the meat. Serve immediately, accompanied by Potato and Parsnip Rösti (see page 100), roast shallots and garlic, steamed mangetout and buttered baby carrots with fresh herbs.

'Hong Kong' Steak Pie with Marinated Pigeon Breast

Marinated Pigeon Breasts:
4 pigeon breasts, skinned
15 ml (1 tbsp) thin honey
5 ml (1 tsp) Chinese five-spice powder
30 ml (2 tbsp) dark soy sauce
15 ml (1 tbsp) oil
10 ml (2 tsp) balsamic vinegar
5 ml (1 tsp) Tabasco sauce

Pie Filling:
350 g (12 oz) braising steak
15 ml (1 tbsp) flour
salt and freshly ground black pepper
15-30 ml (1-2 tbsp) oil
150 ml (¼ pint) water
30-45 ml (2-3 tbsp) fermented salted black beans
30-45 ml (2-3 tbsp) dry sherry
8 pickled walnuts, chopped
5-10 ml (1-2 tsp) Tabasco sauce
225 g (8 oz) button mushrooms, quartered

Pastry:
225 g (8 oz) self-raising flour
125 g (4 oz) shredded suet
150 ml (¼ pint) water (approximately)

1 Place the pigeon breasts in a shallow dish. For the marinade, mix together the remaining ingredients in a bowl, then pour over the breasts. Turn to coat, then leave to marinate for 1-2 hours (no longer or the flavour will be overpowering).

2 For the pie filling, cut the steak into strips and toss in the flour, seasoned with pepper only. Heat the oil in a heavy-based frying pan until smoking, then brown the meat in batches: cook, turning, for a few minutes until evenly browned. Transfer to a 600 ml (1 pint) pie dish or 4 individual pie dishes, using a slotted spoon.

3 Add the water, black beans, sherry and walnuts to the pan. Scrape up the sediment from the bottom of the pan and allow the mixture to come to the boil. Add the Tabasco. Taste to ensure that the flavour is sufficiently pronounced: depending on the strength of the black bean sauce you may need to add more; the Tabasco should add 'kick' without being too fiery.

4 Add the mushrooms to the meat then pour over the sauce, ensuring that the liquid covers the meat; top up with a little water if necessary.

5 To make the pastry dough, mix together the self-raising flour, suet and seasoning in a bowl. Add sufficient water to make a soft dough. Knead lightly until just smooth. Roll out to a 1 cm (½ inch) thickness and use to cover the pie dish(es).

6 Bake in a preheated oven at 180°C (350°F) mark 4 for 40 minutes to 1 hour, depending on the size of your dish.

7 About 10 minutes before serving, preheat a cast-iron griddle or cast-iron frying pan. Add the pigeon breasts and cook for 1-2 minutes on each side. Transfer the breasts to a warmed plate and leave to rest for a few minutes before carving into slices on the diagonal.

8 Serve the steak pie, cut into portions if appropriate, on warmed serving plates and arrange the pigeon breast alongside. Serve at once, with Salud's Cabbage (see page 93) and steamed mangetout.

Fillet of Aberdeen Angus Beef with Buttered Spinach and Parsnip Chips

4 Angus beef fillet steaks, each about
125-175 g (4-6 oz) and 2 cm (¾ inch)
thick
salt and freshly ground black pepper
25 g (1 oz) unsalted butter

Parsnip Chips:
oil for deep-frying
125 g (4 oz) parsnips

Buttered Spinach:
450 g (1 lb) spinach, stalks removed
25 g (1 oz) butter

1 Season the steaks with salt and pepper. Heat the butter in a cast-iron griddle pan until sizzling.

2 Meanwhile, for the chips, heat the oil in a deep-fat fryer and thinly slice the parsnips.

3 Place the steaks in the griddle pan and cook for 2-3 minutes each side, according to taste.

4 In the meantime, cook the spinach with just the water clinging to the leaves after washing and a little seasoning in a tightly covered pan for 3-4 minutes or until just wilted. Add the butter and toss to melt.

5 Whilst cooking the steaks and spinach, deep-fry the parsnips in the hot oil for about 30 seconds to 1 minute until crisp and golden brown. Drain on kitchen paper.

6 Place each steak on a warmed serving plate with a pile of parsnip chips and a mound of buttered spinach. Serve immediately, accompanied by Horseradish Bubble and Squeak (see page 100).

Marinated Fillet of Lamb with a Madeira Sauce

For this recipe, you will need to prepare the stock a day in advance (see below); or up to 1 week ahead if stored in the freezer.

2 whole filleted best ends of lamb, trimmed of all fat
salt and freshly ground black pepper
knob of butter
15-30 ml (1-2 tbsp) groundnut oil

Marinade:
5 shallots, peeled and quartered
2 large rosemary sprigs
12 chives, chopped
3 cloves garlic, sliced
250 ml (8 fl oz) full rich Madeira

Madeira Sauce:
reserved Madeira from the marinade
600 ml (1 pint) homemade stock (see below)
small knob of unsalted butter

1 To marinate the lamb, lay the fillets in a long casserole dish. Sprinkle with the shallots, rosemary, chives and garlic, then pour on the Madeira. Cover and leave to marinate for at least 1½ hours, turning the meat at least once during that time.

2 Lift the meat out of the marinade and pat dry; strain and reserve the marinade. Season the meat with salt and pepper.

3 To make the sauce, put the strained marinade into a pan and simmer to reduce by half. Add the stock and reduce to the required consistency. Check the seasoning, then stir in the knob of unsalted butter.

4 To cook the lamb, heat the butter and a little groundnut oil in a heavy-based frying pan until sizzling. Add the meat and quickly seal on both sides. Turn down the heat and cook for a further 6-8 minutes, depending on the thickness of the meat. Transfer to a warmed plate, cover loosely with foil to keep warm and leave to rest for about 10 minutes.

5 To serve, carve the meat into slices. Arrange on warmed serving plates and pour on the sauce. Serve with Potatoes Dauphinois (see page 103), Roast Parsnip Cups filled with Parsnip Purée (see page 99) and Savoury Spinach with Lamb's Kidneys (see page 90).

Homemade Stock: To make the stock, put 675 g (1½ lb) beef bones and 1.2 kg (2½ lb) lamb bones into a large roasting tin and roast in a preheated oven at 180°C (350°F) mark 4 for 30 minutes. Spread about 150 ml (¼ pint) passata over the bones and add 2 large onions, peeled; 3 leeks; 450 g (1 lb) carrots, peeled; 3 celery sticks and 3 cloves garlic, peeled. Roast for a further 45 minutes.

Using a slotted spoon, transfer the vegetables and bones to a stock pot. Add the bouquet garni and cover with water. Skim the fat off the juices in the roasting tin, then deglaze with a little boiling water and add to the stockpot. Bring to the boil and simmer for 3-4 hours, skimming off any fat and residue that rises to the surface. Strain through a large colander, then several times through a muslin-lined sieve.

Transfer the stock to a clean pan and reduce to just over 600 ml (1 pint). Pour into a jug and allow to cool, then chill in the refrigerator, until required. It will set to a solid jelly.

Boned Saddle of Welsh Lamb filled and topped with Crab Soufflé, served with a Tarragon and Red Wine Sauce

1 whole saddle of Welsh lamb, about 2 kg (4½ lb), boned
salt

Marinade:
1 onion, chopped
1 garlic clove, crushed
60 ml (2 fl oz) olive oil
4-5 tarragon sprigs
freshly ground black pepper

Crab Soufflé:
150 ml (¼ pint) milk
1 onion slice
1 mace blade
small piece of fresh nutmeg
25 g (1 oz) butter
15 g (½ oz) plain flour
225 g (8 oz) fresh crab meat (mostly white meat)
5 ml (1 tsp) paprika
few drops of Tabasco or other hot pepper sauce
30 ml (2 tbsp) double cream
2 eggs (size 2), separated
dried breadcrumbs, for sprinkling

Tarragon and Red Wine Sauce:
600 ml (1 pint) well-flavoured brown veal or beef stock, clarified
2 small bunches of tarragon, leaves only
150 ml (¼ pint) red wine
5 ml (1 tsp) arrowroot, blended with a little cold water
a little tomato purée (optional)
salt and freshly ground black pepper

To Garnish:
dill sprigs
small crab claws
tarragon leaves
strips of roasted red pepper

1 Place the lamb in a large shallow dish. Add the ingredients for the marinade and turn the meat to coat. Leave to marinate in a cool place for at least 30 minutes, preferably overnight.

2 To prepare the soufflé, put the milk in a saucepan with the onion, mace and nutmeg. Slowly bring almost to the boil, then remove from the heat and leave to infuse. Melt half of the butter in another pan, stir in the flour and cook, stirring, for 1 minute. Remove from the heat. Strain the milk and gradually stir into the roux. Return to the heat and cook, stirring constantly, until thickened. Set aside.

3 Pound the crab meat, using a mortar and pestle, to release its flavour. Melt the remaining 15 g (½ oz) butter in a pan, add the paprika and Tabasco and heat briefly. Remove from the heat, stir in the crab meat and season with salt and pepper. Return to the heat and stir in the béchamel sauce and cream. Let cool slightly, then beat in the egg yolks and set aside to cool. (The soufflé mixture can be made ahead to this stage and refrigerated until required.)

4 To make the tarragon and red wine sauce, heat the stock in a small pan and add the tarragon leaves. Stand in a bain-marie and leave to infuse and reduce slightly over a very low heat for 30 minutes or more. In another pan, boil the red wine to reduce to 15 ml (1 tbsp). Stir in the blended arrowroot, then stir into the stock. Cook, stirring, until the sauce is slightly thickened and clear. Check the seasoning and correct the colour with a little tomato purée if required.

5 Oil four 7.5 cm (2 inch) and four 3 cm (1¼ inch) metal rings, which are approximately 3 cm (1¼ inch) deep. Dust with breadcrumbs. Remove the lamb from the marinade, pat dry and cut into 2.5 cm (1 inch) pieces. Fit the lamb into the larger rings, arranging the pieces upright so they fit snugly, three quarters of the way round each ring; fill the gap with a piece of crumpled foil. (This will later be filled with the soufflé.)

6 Season the meat well with salt. Heat an ovenproof non-stick cast iron skillet or frying pan and carefully lift the rings into it. Cook over a high heat for a few minutes on each side to sear the meat on both sides, using a fish slice to carefully turn the rings once.

7 Meanwhile, finish the soufflé preparation. Whisk the egg whites to soft peaks. Stir a spoonful into the crab mixture to lighten it, then gently fold in the rest.

8 Take the skillet or frying pan off the heat and remove the foil. Fill the spaces with some of the soufflé mixture, spreading it over the meat as well, and heaping it up slightly. Stand the smaller rings in the skillet or frying pan, and fill these with the remaining soufflé mixture. Level the tops and sprinkle with breadcrumbs. Place the frying pan in a preheated oven at 200°C (400°F) mark 6 and bake for 15 minutes or until the meat is tender but still pink inside and the soufflés are risen and browned.

9 To serve, reheat the sauce, then pour a pool on to each warmed serving plate. Unmould the lamb onto the plates, positioning it slightly off centre. Unmould the crab soufflés, place to one side of the lamb and garnish with dill. Garnish the plate with small crab claws, tarragon leaves and strips of roasted red pepper. Serve with Baby Potato Kebabs (see page 106), Julienne Leek Bundles (see page 88), and a medley of steamed beans (such as runner, French, wax and Blue Kentucky, as available.)

Fillet of Lamb on a Root Vegetable Plinth

1 boned loin of lamb, about 600 g (1¼ lb)
150 ml (¼ pint) port
30 ml (2 tbsp) oil
250 ml (8 fl oz) brown stock
shredded zest and juice of 1-2 lemons

Vegetable Plinth:
200 g (7 oz) carrots
200 g (7 oz) parsnips
200 g (7 oz) potatoes
200 g (7 oz) turnip
200 g (7 oz) sweet potato
2 eggs
100 ml (3½ fl oz) double cream
2 cloves garlic, crushed
30 g (1¼ oz) spring onions, finely chopped
30 g (1¼ oz) finely chopped parsley
salt and freshly ground black pepper

1 Ensure that the lamb is trimmed of all fat and sinew. Place in a shallow dish, pour the port over the meat and leave to marinate for 2 hours.

2 Meanwhile, prepare the vegetables. Cut all the root vegetables into strips, about 5 cm (2 inches) long and about 5-10 mm (¼-½ inch) in diameter. Cook in lightly salted boiling water for about 10-12 minutes. Drain and leave to cool.

3 Beat the eggs in a bowl, then mix in the cream. Add the garlic, spring onions and parsley. Season with salt and pepper to taste.

4 Add the vegetable strips to the cream mixture and mix gently together, taking care not to mash or break the vegetable strips. Using a palette knife, shape the mixture into an oblong on a large greased baking tray. Bake in a preheated oven at 190°C (375°F) mark 5 for 20-25 minutes until golden.

5 Remove the meat from the marinade, reserving the marinade. Heat the oil in a heavy-based pan. When hot, add the whole piece of lamb and fry over a high heat for about 4 minutes, turning regularly to ensure that the whole surface is sealed and browned. Remove, cover and leave to rest in a warm place.

6 Add the stock, reserved marinade, lemon zest and juice to the pan. Bring almost to the boil and simmer until reduced by half. Check the seasoning.

7 To serve, cut the vegetable oblong into 4 plinths and place one in the centre of each serving plate. Cut the lamb into thick slices and arrange on top, then pour over the port and lemon gravy. Serve with Raspberried Red Cabbage (see page 91) and Stuffed Savoy Cabbage (see page 92).

Roast Rack of Lamb with a Rosemary and Port Sauce

For this recipe, ask your butcher to French trim the racks of lamb, removing all fat and sinews between the bones down to the 'eye' of the meat.

2 whole best ends of lamb, fat removed and French trimmed
olive oil, for cooking
sea salt and freshly ground black pepper
4 rosemary sprigs
3-4 cloves garlic, peeled

Rosemary and Port Sauce:
300 ml (½ pint) lamb stock
60 ml (4 tbsp) port
2 rosemary sprigs
50 g (2 oz) butter, chilled and diced

Croûtes:
4 slices bread
30 ml (2 tbsp) chopped parsley

1 Brush the racks of lamb with olive oil and season with salt and pepper. Heat a little olive oil in a large heavy-based frying pan and sear the meat over a high heat on all sides.

2 Lay the rosemary sprigs and garlic cloves in a roasting tin and place the lamb racks on top (reserving the juices in the pan). Roast in a preheated oven at 200°C (400°F) mark 6 for 12-14 minutes, until tender but still pink in the middle.

3 Meanwhile, make the sauce. Put the lamb stock in a saucepan with the reserved pan juices. Add the port and rosemary sprigs and boil for about 5 minutes to reduce. Lower the heat and whisk in the butter, a piece at a time, to thicken the sauce and give it a glossy finish.

4 When the lamb is cooked, cover and leave to rest in a warm place for 5 minutes. In the meantime, cut a 7.5 cm (3 inch) round from each slice of bread, using a suitable pastry cutter. Heat a thin layer of olive oil in a frying pan and shallow-fry the bread rounds until crisp and golden on both sides. Drain on kitchen paper, then dip the croûtes in chopped parsley to coat.

5 To serve, place a parsley croûte in the centre of each warmed serving plate and arrange 3 lamb cutlets on top. Surround with the sauce and garnish with rosemary. Serve with Carrots with Cumin (see page 94) and Anna Potatoes (see page 105).

Grilled Fillet of Lamb with Spiced Couscous

4 best-end of neck lamb fillets, each about
200 g (7 oz)
salt and freshly ground black pepper

Marinade:
60 ml (4 tbsp) olive oil
30 ml (2 tbsp) lemon juice
30 ml (2 tbsp) coriander seeds, crushed

Couscous:
1 medium aubergine, finely diced
90 ml (6 tbsp) olive oil
2.5 ml (½ tsp) ground cumin
1 onion, finely chopped
1 clove garlic, finely chopped
10 ml (2 tsp) ground mixed spice
250 ml (9 fl oz) tomato juice
200 g (7 oz) couscous
1 courgette, finely diced
finely grated zest of 2 lemons
1 bunch coriander, leaves finely chopped
(stalks reserved)

For the Jus:
600 ml (1 pint) lamb stock
reserved coriander stalks

1 Lay the lamb fillets in a shallow dish and drizzle over the olive oil and lemon juice. Turn the fillets to coat, then sprinkle with the crushed coriander seeds and season with salt and pepper. Cover and leave to marinate in a cool place for 1-2 hours.

2 For the couscous, put the diced aubergine in a small baking tin, drizzle over 60 ml (4 tbsp) of the olive oil and sprinkle with the ground cumin. Season with salt and pepper to taste. Roast in a preheated oven at 200°C (400°F) mark 6 for about 12-15 minutes until lightly browned.

3 Meanwhile, heat the remaining olive oil in a large saucepan, add the onion and fry until softened and golden brown. Add the garlic and mixed spice and fry for a few seconds more. Pour in the tomato juice and bring to the boil.

4 Add the couscous, roasted aubergine, courgette and grated lemon zest. Toss well and season with salt and pepper to taste. Cover and leave to stand in a warm place for at least 15 minutes for the couscous to soften.

5 Meanwhile, preheat a ridged griddle pan, add the lamb fillets and cook over a medium-high heat for about 15-20 minutes, until tender but still pink in the middle. Cover and leave to rest in a warm place for 10 minutes before carving.

6 In the meantime make the jus. Bring the stock to the boil in a pan and reduce by half. Add the coriander stalks and leave to infuse for 10 minutes. Strain through a fine sieve and reheat.

7 To serve, carve each lamb fillet into 5 or 6 slices. Add the chopped coriander to the couscous and fork through. Pile some couscous into the centre of each warmed serving plate and arrange the lamb around it. Spoon over the jus and serve at once.

Note: During the summer, this lamb is exceptionally good cooked over a charcoal barbecue.

Fillet of Lamb with Port and Mulberry Sauce

*2 whole best end of lamb fillets, trimmed of
all fat and sinew*
4 shallots, peeled
2 knobs of butter
15 ml (1 tbsp) light olive oil

Sauce:
225 g (8 oz) mulberries (see note)
900 ml (1½ pints) lamb stock
60 ml (2 fl oz) port
salt and freshly ground black pepper

To Garnish:
rosemary sprigs

1 Place the shallots in an ovenproof dish with a knob of butter and cook in a preheated oven at 160°C (325°F) mark 3 for 1½ hours until caramelised.

2 Meanwhile, make the sauce. Crush the mulberries, then press through a fine nylon sieve into a bowl.

3 Bring the lamb stock to the boil in a heavy-based pan and reduce by three quarters, then add the mulberry juice and half of the port. Reduce by half, then add the rest of the port. Adjust the seasoning, pass through a fine sieve into a clean pan and keep warm.

4 Heat the oil and remaining butter in a heavy-based frying pan. Add the lamb fillets and seal over a high heat, turning until evenly browned on all sides. Transfer to a roasting tin and cook in a preheated oven at 200°C (400°F) mark 6 for 12-15 minutes for rare meat; a little longer for medium. Remove from the oven, cover with foil and leave to rest in a warm place for 5 minutes.

5 To serve, carve the meat into slices and arrange on warmed serving plates. Pour the sauce around one side of each plate; arrange the caramelised shallots and rosemary sprig on the other side. Serve at once, with Baked Cabbage scented with Garlic and Juniper (see page 93) and Julienne of Honey-glazed Carrots (see page 94)

Note: If mulberries are unobtainable, use blackberries instead.

Rosettes of Lamb with a Potato and Parsnip Rösti Crust and a Wine and Redcurrant Sauce

175 g (6 oz) potato, such as Maris Piper
2 parsnips
2 whole best end of lamb fillets, trimmed of
    all fat and sinew
2 garlic cloves, crushed
salt and freshly ground black pepper
plain flour, for dusting
2 egg yolks
15 ml (1 tbsp) vegetable oil
25 g (1 oz) unsalted butter

Sauce:
25 g (1 oz) shallots, chopped
275 ml (9 fl oz) Cabernet Sauvignon
250 ml (8 fl oz) lamb stock
2 rosemary sprigs
30-45 ml (2-3 tbsp) redcurrant jelly
5 ml (1 tsp) cornflour, mixed with a little
    water (optional)

To Garnish:
redcurrants
rosemary sprigs

1 Peel and halve the potato and parsnips. Par-boil in water for about 7 minutes. Drain and cool.

2 Cut each lamb fillet into 4-6 rosettes, depending on size. Rub all over with the crushed garlic. Season with salt and pepper and dust with flour; set aside.

3 To prepare the rösti crust, grate the potatoes and parsnips into a bowl (avoiding the 'woody' centre of the parsnips). Add the egg yolks and seasoning; mix well. Place a spoonful of the rösti mixture on each lamb rosette and press down firmly. Refrigerate until required.

4 Heat the oil and butter in a heavy-based frying pan and fry the lamb rosettes in batches, on both sides until golden brown. Transfer the lamb to a baking tray and cook in a preheated oven at 200°C (400°F) mark 6 for about 8-10 minutes, until browned on the outside but still pink in the middle; keep warm.

5 Meanwhile make the sauce. Pour off most of the fat from the frying pan, add the shallots and sweat until softened. Add the wine and let bubble until reduced by half. Add the stock, rosemary sprigs and redcurrant jelly to taste. Reduce to the desired consistency, adding the cornflour to thicken if necessary. Check the seasoning and pass through a fine sieve.

6 Remove the string from the lamb and arrange on warmed serving plates. Garnish with the redcurrants and rosemary. Serve accompanied by Parsnip Crisps (see page 98), Glazed Baby Carrots (see page 94) and Caramelised Shallots (see page 96).

Pan-fried Fillet of Lamb with Rosemary, Roasted Aubergine and Garlic, Caramelised Plum Tomatoes and Couscous

1 best end of lamb fillet, about 600 g (1¼ lb)
60 ml (4 tbsp) olive oil (not extra-virgin)
few rosemary sprigs, leaves only
salt and freshly ground black pepper

Roasted Aubergine and Garlic:
1 long, thin aubergine, thinly sliced
8 cloves garlic
olive oil, for drizzling

Caramelised Plum Tomatoes:
4 plum tomatoes, quartered lengthwise
30 ml (2 tbsp) extra-virgin olive oil
7.5 ml (1½ tsp) caster sugar
15 ml (1 tbsp) balsamic vinegar
150 ml (¼ pint) homemade jellied lamb stock

Couscous:
15 ml (1 tbsp) olive oil
pinch of freshly grated nutmeg
pinch each of ground cinnamon, coriander,
  cumin and ginger
4 shallots, sliced into rounds
225 g (8 oz) couscous
150 ml (¼ pint) hot jellied lamb stock
300 ml (½ pint) boiling water
15 ml (1 tbsp) roasted garlic-flavoured olive oil
  (see note)
15 ml (1 tbsp) chopped flat-leaf parsley
15-30 ml (1-2 tbsp) skinned pistachio nuts

1 First prepare the roasted aubergine and garlic. Sprinkle the aubergine slices with salt. Place in a colander, cover with a saucer and weight down. Leave to degorge for 30 minutes. Blanch the garlic cloves in a pan of boiling water for 5 minutes. Rinse the aubergine slices and pat dry. Place on an oiled baking tray with the garlic cloves and sprinkle liberally with olive oil. Roast in a preheated oven at 175°C (335°F) mark 3½ for 45 minutes.

2 For the caramelised tomatoes, heat the olive oil in a frying pan. Add the tomatoes and sizzle for about 3 minutes, then add the sugar and balsamic vinegar. Simmer for about 5-10 minutes until the tomatoes are just cooked, but still holding their shape. Remove from the pan with a slotted spoon; set aside in a warm place. Add the lamb stock to the pan and boil to reduce by about half. Season and reserve this jus.

3 For the couscous, heat the 15 ml (1 tbsp) olive oil in a heavy-based frying pan with the spices. As soon as the spices begin to release their aroma, add the shallots and fry until softened but not browned. Put the couscous into a bowl. In a measuring jug, mix the lamb stock and boiling water together and add the 15 ml (1 tbsp) roasted garlic olive oil. Pour this liquid over the couscous, cover and let stand for 5 minutes. Transfer the plumped up couscous to a steamer and steam over boiling water for 20 minutes.

4 To cook the lamb, heat the olive oil in a heavy-based frying pan over a high heat. Add the lamb with the rosemary leaves and cook for 7-8 minutes until browned and crispy on the outside, but still pink inside. Season with salt and pepper to taste. Reheat the shallots, add the parsley and pistachio nuts, then mix with the couscous.

5 Slice the lamb and arrange on a bed of roasted aubergine and garlic, with the caramelised tomatoes and couscous. Drizzle the jus over the tomatoes and serve at once.

Note: You can buy olive oil flavoured with roasted garlic, or make your own by infusing roasted garlic cloves in olive oil.

Bacon and Parsley Dumpling on a Hot Apple, Walnut, and Fennel Salad, with a Tarragon-scented Tomato Sauce

Suet Pastry:
300 g (10 oz) self-raising flour
150 g (5 oz) shredded vegetable suet
pinch of salt
200 ml (⅓ pint) water (approximately)

Filling:
15 ml (1 tbsp) extra-virgin olive oil
200 g (7 oz) maple-cured streaky bacon, finely chopped
1 large onion, finely diced
1 large bunch flat-leaf parsley, stalks removed, finely chopped
salt and freshly ground black pepper

Tarragon-scented Tomato Sauce:
30 ml (2 tbsp) extra-virgin olive oil
1 large onion, finely chopped
1 clove garlic, finely chopped
20 ml (4 tsp) tomato purée
400 g (14 oz) can plum tomatoes
few tarragon leaves, finely chopped
small bunch of basil leaves, finely chopped
dash of white wine vinegar
pinch of sugar, to taste
salt and freshly ground black pepper

Hot Apple Salad:
15 g (½ oz) unsalted butter
70 g (2½ oz) walnut halves
1 large fennel bulb, finely sliced
1 Granny Smith apple, cored and sliced
1 small Cos lettuce, stems removed and chopped
salt and freshly ground black pepper

To Garnish:
parsley sprigs

1 To prepare the pastry, combine the flour, suet and salt in a mixing bowl. Add sufficient water to make a firm dough, mixing with a round-bladed knife. (The amount of water can only be an approximation as it will depend upon the absorption of the flour.) Leave the dough to rest for 15 minutes.

2 Heat the oil in a heavy-based frying pan. Add the bacon and cook, stirring, over a medium heat for 2 minutes. Add the onion and cook until softened. Remove from the heat and stir in the chopped parsley. Season with salt and pepper to taste and leave to cool.

3 Divide the dough into 4 even portions. Roll out each piece to a rectangle about 23 x 15 cm (9 x 6 inches). Divide the bacon mixture evenly between the 4 sheets of dough leaving a 2.5 cm (1 inch) border free along the edges. Moisten the pastry edges with water. Roll up each one from the long end, sealing the edges as you do so. Wrap loosely in cling film and refrigerate until needed. Bring the water in a steamer to the boil. Place the puddings in the steamer, and cook for approximately 1 hour.

4 To make the tomato sauce, heat the oil in a pan, add the onion and garlic and fry until softened. Stir in the tomato purée, then add the tomatoes and herbs. Stir well and continue to cook over a low heat for 10 minutes. (If necessary, thin the sauce with a little hot water.) Add the vinegar and season with sugar, salt and pepper to taste. Purée in a blender or food processor, then pass through a sieve. Reheat if necessary before serving.

5 Prepare the salad about 5 minutes before the dumplings will be ready. Melt the butter in a heavy-based saucepan over a medium heat. Add the walnuts and fry for

2 minutes, stirring occasionally. Add the fennel and cook for a further 2 minutes. Add the apple and cook for 1 minute. Add the chopped lettuce and cook until it is wilted. Season with salt and pepper to taste.

6 Divide the hot salad between individual serving plates. Halve each dumpling and arrange on top of the salad. Pour the sauce around the dumplings and serve at once, garnished with parsley.

Pork wrapped in Spinach and Bacon with a Mushroom Stuffing

575 g (1¼ lb) pork tenderloin
450 g (1 lb) spinach (about 30 leaves)
20 g (¾ oz) dried porcini mushrooms
45 ml (3 tbsp) olive oil
1 clove garlic, crushed
10 ml (2 tsp) dried sage
175 g (6 oz) chestnut mushrooms, chopped
salt and freshly ground black pepper
12 thin-cut rashers unsmoked streaky bacon

1 Cut the pork tenderloin into 6-8 strips of even length and cut each strip in half.

2 Blanch the spinach leaves in a micro-wave with just the water clinging to the leaves after washing for 30 seconds. Alternatively cook in a saucepan for 30 seconds to 1 minute until softened. Drain thoroughly. Wrap the pork tenderloin strips in the spinach leaves, ensuring that each strip is completely covered.

3 Soak the porcini mushrooms in hot water to cover for 10 minutes. Drain, reserving the soaking liquid. Pass the liquid through a fine sieve to remove any grit.

4 Heat the olive oil in a frying pan with the garlic and sage. Add the chestnut mushrooms and porcini, together with 45-60 ml (3-4 tbsp) of the liquid. Add a further 45-60 ml (3-4 tbsp) liquid, then reduce the mixture until there is little liquid remaining and the mushrooms are cooked. Season with salt and pepper to taste. Transfer the mixture to a food processor and process until it is the consistency of a paté.

5 Lay 6 rashers of bacon side by side on a clean surface, overlapping them slightly to form a 'sheet'. Spread a quarter of the mushroom mixture across the middle and place 3-4 of the spinach-wrapped pork pieces horizontally across the bacon on top of the mushroom mixture. Spread another quarter of the mushroom mixture on top of the pork. Wrap the bacon pieces around the pork and place on an oiled baking tray, join-side down.

6 Repeat the process with the remaining bacon, pork and mushroom mixture so that you have 2 bacon-wrapped 'joints' on the baking tray. Roast in a preheated oven at 200°C (400°F) mark 6 for 20-25 minutes or until the bacon is cooked and crispy.

7 Remove from the oven and cut into slices, using a sharp knife. Carefully transfer to warmed serving plates, using a fish slice. Serve accompanied by Parsnip Purée with Parmesan (see page 99), broccoli and spinach.

Fillet of Pork with Prunes

For this recipe you will need to soak the prunes overnight.

12 prunes
450 ml (¾ pint) dry white wine
700 g (1½ lb) pork fillet
plain flour, for coating
salt and freshly ground black pepper
50 g (2 oz) salted butter (approximately)
30 ml (2 tbsp) olive oil
30 ml (2 tbsp) redcurrant jelly
175 ml (6 fl oz) double cream
sage leaves, to garnish

1 Rinse the prunes under cold running water, then place in a small bowl and pour on 300 ml (½ pint) of the wine. Cover and leave to soak overnight.

2 Transfer the prunes and soaking liquid to a small pan and simmer for 10-15 minutes. Remove from the heat; keep warm.

3 Meanwhile, trim the pork fillet and cut on the diagonal into 2.5 cm (1 inch) thick pieces. Lay the pieces on a board and flatten slightly with a rolling pin or meat mallet. Season the flour with salt and pepper and spread on a plate. Toss the pork pieces in the flour to coat, shaking off excess.

4 Heat the butter and oil in a frying pan. Brown the pieces of pork a few at a time; remove with a slotted spoon and set aside. Add more butter to the pan as you fry the later batches, if needed.

5 Return all the browned meat to the pan. Add the rest of the wine and let bubble for a few minutes. Lower the heat and simmer, covered, for 20 minutes until tender.

6 Lift out the pork with a slotted spoon, place in a covered dish and keep warm. Drain the prunes, adding the soaking wine to the frying pan. Boil until reduced, then add the redcurrant jelly and stir until dissolved. Add the cream and reduce until the sauce is thick enough to thinly coat the back of the spoon. Add the cooked prunes.

7 Arrange the pork slices on warmed serving plates and surround with the sauce. Serve immediately, garnished with sage leaves and accompanied by Creamed Polenta (see page 108) and Broccoli with Crisp Pancetta (see page 89).

Note: If you prefer to add more gloss to the sauce whisk in a few knobs of butter before adding the prunes.

Accompaniments

Spinach and Cucumber Ribbons

1 cucumber
450 g (1 lb) large spinach leaves

1 Using a swivel vegetable peeler, pare ribbons from the length of the cucumber, rotating the cucumber as you do so. Roll the cucumber ribbons into nest shapes.

2 Wash the spinach and drain thoroughly. Stack the leaves in piles, then roll them up and slice into fine ribbons, using a sharp knife. Form into nest shapes.

3 Bring the water to the boil in the base of a steamer. Put the cucumber and spinach nests in the steamer and steam for 4-5 minutes until the spinach has just wilted. Serve at once.

Julienne Leek Bundles

450 g (1 lb) leeks, cleaned
salt
melted clarified butter, for brushing

1 Cut the white part of the leeks from the green part and set aside. Cut at least 8 ribbons from the green leaves and reserve for tying the bundles. Discard the rest of the green leaves.

2 Halve the white parts lengthwise, then cut into 6 cm (2½ inch) lengths. Cut into julienne strips. Divide the julienne into bundles and tie a green 'leek ribbon' around each bundle. Season with salt and place in a steamer over boiling water for 4-5 minutes, until just softening.

3 Transfer to a warmed serving dish and brush with the melted butter to serve.

Glazed Green Beans

225 g (8 oz) fine green beans, trimmed
salt and freshly ground black pepper
15 g (½ oz) butter
30 ml (2 tbsp) water

1 Add the beans to a large pan of boiling salted water and cook for 2-3 minutes. Drain and refresh under cold running water. Place in a bowl of cold water and set aside.

2 When ready to serve, drain the beans. Melt the butter with the 30 ml (2 tbsp) of water, a pinch of salt and a few turns of pepper. Add the beans, bring to the boil, cover and cook for 1 minute.

3 Remove the lid and cook for a further 1 minute until the beans are glazed. Taste and adjust the seasoning. Serve at once.

Green Beans in Minted Vinaigrette

125 g (4 oz) green beans
15 ml (1 tbsp) olive oil
5 ml (1 tsp) balsamic vinegar
7.5 ml (1½ tsp) chopped mint
salt and freshly ground black pepper

1 Put the beans into a steamer and steam over boiling water for about 4 minutes, or until just cooked. Meanwhile, put the olive oil, vinegar and mint in a small pan and heat through.

2 Drain the beans and toss with the warm vinaigrette. Season with salt and pepper. Serve at once.

Broccoli with Crisp Pancetta

450 g (1 lb) broccoli, cut into florets
6-8 slices of pancetta, cut into 1 cm (½ inch)
  squares
30 ml (2 tbsp) olive oil
50 g (2 oz) pine nuts

1 Par-cook the broccoli in a steamer over boiling water for about 3-4 minutes until almost cooked but still quite crunchy; take care to avoid overcooking.

2 In the meantime, dry-fry the pancetta in a heavy-based frying pan until crisp; remove and set aside. Add the olive oil to the frying pan and fry the pine nuts until golden brown; remove with a slotted spoon.

3 Drain the broccoli, add to the frying pan and stir-fry for 2-3 minutes. Add the pine nuts and toss to mix. Transfer to a warmed serving dish and top with the crispy pancetta.

Broccoli Timbales

450 g (1 lb) broccoli, cut into florets
  (including stalks)
90 ml (3 fl oz) double cream
1 egg (size 2)
2.5 ml (½ tsp) freshly grated nutmeg
salt and freshly ground black pepper

1 Place the broccoli in a steamer over boiling water, cover and steam for about 5 minutes until *just* tender and still bright green. Refresh in cold water; drain thoroughly.

2 Put the broccoli in a food processor or blender with the cream, egg, nutmeg, and salt and pepper to taste. Process until smooth.

3 Divide the mixture evenly between four greased individual 150 ml (¼ pint) metal pudding basins or dariole moulds. Cook in a preheated oven at 180°C (350°F) mark 4 for 20 minutes.

4 Turn out onto warmed plates and serve at once.

Three-colour Vegetable Stir-fry

1 red pepper, halved, cored and seeded
1 green pepper, halved, cored and seeded
1 carrot, peeled
15 ml (1 tbsp) sesame oil
salt and freshly ground black pepper

1 Thinly slice each vegetable into strips.

2 Heat the oil in a wok or frying pan and add the vegetables, with salt and pepper to taste. Fry over a high heat, stirring constantly for about 3-4 minutes until the vegetables are tender, but not soft. Serve immediately.

Spinach Purée with Pine Nuts

350 g (12 oz) spinach, stalks removed
4-5 dill sprigs, leaves only
salt
25 g (1 oz) pine nuts

1 Put the spinach into a saucepan with just the water clinging to the leaves after washing. Add the dill and a little salt and cook until the spinach is wilted.

2 Drain off most of the water from the spinach, then purée in a blender or food processor. Add the pine nuts and work briefly to chop the nuts into smaller pieces. Drain off any excess liquid and keep warm until ready to serve.

Buttered Spinach with Nutmeg

450 g (1 lb) spinach, stalks removed
30 g (1 oz) unsalted butter
freshly grated nutmeg
salt and freshly ground black pepper

1 Put the spinach into a saucepan with just the water clinging to the leaves after washing. Add the butter, nutmeg, salt and pepper to taste. Cover and cook until just wilted.

2 Check the seasoning and serve at once.

Savoury Spinach with Lamb's Kidneys

225 g (8 oz) spinach leaves
salt and freshly ground black pepper
15 g (½ oz) butter
5 shallots, finely chopped
1 plump clove garlic, crushed
5 ml (1 tsp) dried marjoram
2 lamb's kidneys, cored and finely chopped
small bunch of chives, chopped

1 Preheat a heavy-based frying pan, add the spinach with just the water clinging to the leaves after washing and a little salt. Cook, stirring, for 1-2 minutes, then drain thoroughly in a sieve, pressing out excess moisture. Set aside.

2 Melt the butter in the frying pan, add the shallots and garlic and sauté until softened, but not brown. Add the marjoram and chopped kidneys and cook for 4-5 minutes, until the kidney is cooked. Add the chives, spinach and pepper to taste. Stir well, heat through and check the seasoning. Serve at once.

Raspberried Red Cabbage

400 g (14 oz) red cabbage, cored
100 ml (3½ fl oz) water
15 ml (1 tbsp) lemon juice
50 ml (2 fl oz) raspberry vinegar
25 g (1 oz) sugar
pinch of salt
25 g (1 oz) butter

1 Place the red cabbage in a saucepan with the water, lemon juice, vinegar, sugar and salt. Bring to the boil and simmer for about 15 minutes until just tender. Remove the lid and allow to bubble until any excess liquid has evaporated.

2 Add the butter and toss before serving.

Spicy Red Cabbage with Apple

2 baby red cabbages, halved and cored
1 cooking apple, peeled
300 ml (½ pint) unsweetened apple juice
30 ml (2 tbsp) demerara sugar
15 ml (1 tbsp) fennel seeds
salt and freshly ground black pepper
25 g (1 oz) butter, in pieces

1 Finely slice the red cabbages and place in a well-buttered casserole dish.

2 Grate the apple and place in a separate bowl. Toss with the apple juice.

3 Sprinkle the sugar and fennel seeds over the cabbage and season with salt and pepper to taste. Pour the apple mixture over the cabbage and stir to mix. Dot with the butter. Cover and cook in a preheated oven at 180°C (350°F) mark 4 for 1 hour, stirring occasionally during cooking. Serve hot or cold.

Braised Cabbage Rolls

40 ml (2½ tbsp) vegetable oil
1 garlic clove, finely chopped
1 shallot, finely chopped
100 g (3½ oz) smoked bacon, derinded and diced
1 baby white cabbage, cored and finely shredded
300 ml (½ pint) chicken stock
4 large Savoy cabbage leaves

1 Heat the oil in a large pan, add the garlic, shallot and bacon and fry until the bacon is golden. Add the cabbage and sweat until most of the liquid has evaporated. Add the stock and bring to the boil. Simmer over a low heat for 25-30 minutes until tender.

2 Meanwhile, blanch the 4 large Savoy cabbage leaves in boiling salted water until pliable. Drain thoroughly and cut out any tough central veins; lay the leaves flat on a clean surface.

3 Drain off any excess liquid from the braised cabbage, then place a generous spoonful at one end of each Savoy leaf. Roll up, folding in the edges to seal. Place, seam-side down, in a warmed ovenproof dish. Warm through in the oven just prior to serving.

Stuffed Savoy Cabbage

1 large Savoy cabbage
25 g (1 oz) butter
50 g (2 oz) chopped walnuts
freshly grated nutmeg
salt and freshly ground black pepper

1 Discard any damaged or discoloured leaves from the cabbage, then select the 4 best, largest, outer leaves. Blanch these in a large pan of boiling salted water for 2 minutes until pliable. Lift out the leaves, using a slotted spoon and reserve the liquid. Immediately rinse the blanched leaves under cold water to prevent further cooking. Drain and pat dry with kitchen paper.

2 Finely shred the white heart of the cabbage and blanch in the reserved liquid for about 1 minute. Drain, reserving the liquid, and mix the cabbage with the butter, walnuts and nutmeg. Season with salt and pepper to taste.

3 Lay the blanched whole green leaves out on a clean surface and place a large spoonful of the shredded cabbage mixture in the centre of each one. Wrap the leaves around the filling to form parcels.

4 Bring the reserved cooking water to the boil in the base of a steamer. Place the cabbage parcels in the steamer and steam for 5-10 minutes. Serve at once.

Baked Cabbage Scented with Garlic and Juniper

225 g (8 oz) Savoy cabbage, cored
salt
15-20 juniper berries
knob of butter
4 large cloves garlic, peeled

1 Finely shred the cabbage and place in a bowl of cold salted water.

2 Crush 7 or 8 juniper berries and add to the cabbage. Leave to stand for about 1 hour, then drain thoroughly.

3 Prick the rest of the juniper berries with the point of a sharp knife and soak in a small bowl of hot water for a few minutes; drain.

4 Take a large double thickness square of kitchen foil and spread with a knob of butter. Pile the cabbage, juniper berries and garlic in the middle. Fold the foil around the cabbage to enclose and seal the parcel tightly. Bake in a preheated oven at 200°C (400°F) mark 6 for 20 minutes.

5 Unwrap and serve the cabbage on warmed side plates.

Salud's Cabbage

125 g (4 oz) rindless streaky bacon, finely diced
15 ml (1 tbsp) oil
2 cloves garlic, finely sliced
¼ firm green or white cabbage, cored and very finely shredded
15 ml (1 tbsp) light soy sauce

1 Dry-fry the bacon in a deep frying pan or wok until crispy, then remove with a slotted spoon and drain on kitchen paper.

2 Add the oil to the pan and heat, then add the garlic and cook until golden brown. Add the cabbage to the pan and stir to coat with the oil. Cook, stirring continuously, until the cabbage just begins to wilt.

3 Add the soy sauce and cook for 1-2 minutes; do not allow the cabbage to become too soft.

4 To serve, scatter the bacon pieces over the cabbage.

Julienne of Honey-glazed Carrots

225 g (8 oz) carrots, peeled
15 ml (1 tbsp) well-flavoured honey
25 g (1 oz) butter
60 ml (2 fl oz) water

1 Cut the carrots into long julienne strips.

2 Combine the honey, butter and water in a heavy-based pan and heat gently until melted. Increase the heat and bring to the boil.

3 Add the carrots, cover with a tight-fitting lid and shake the pan to coat the carrots with the glaze.

4 Return to the heat and cook, covered, over a medium-high heat for 5 minutes.

5 Drain and serve the carrots on warmed side plates.

Carrots with Cumin

700 g (1½ lb) carrots
50 g (2 oz) butter
10 ml (2 tsp) cumin seeds, lightly crushed
juice of 1 lemon
salt and freshly ground black pepper

1 Peel and grate the carrots.

2 Melt the butter in a saucepan, add the cumin and fry gently for 2 minutes.

3 Add the carrots and lemon juice to the pan. Cover and simmer gently for 10-15 minutes. Season with salt and pepper to taste before serving.

Glazed Baby Carrots

25 g (1 oz) unsalted butter
12 baby carrots, trimmed with a little green left on if possible
25 g (1 oz) caster sugar
salt and freshly ground black pepper

1 Melt the butter in a pan, and add the carrots and sugar. Cook for 2-3 minutes.

2 Half-cover with water, put a lid on the pan and simmer for about 5 minutes until cooked, but still firm. Season lightly and keep warm until ready to serve.

Lemon-glazed Carrot Ribbons

4 carrots, peeled
25 g (1 oz) unsalted butter
15 ml (1 tbsp) caster sugar
grated zest of ½ lemon
salt and freshly ground black pepper
1 small lemon balm sprig, finely chopped

1 Using a swivel potato peeler, pare the carrots into long thin ribbons. Blanch in a large pan of boiling water for 15 seconds; drain thoroughly.

2 Heat the butter and sugar in a saucepan until very hot. Add the carrots and stir-fry for 2 minutes. Add the lemon zest and season with salt and pepper to taste.

3 Add the chopped lemon balm and toss to mix. Serve immediately.

Tiered Shredded Vegetable Crowns

180 g (6 oz) courgettes
180 g (6 oz) carrot
180 g (6 oz) parsnip
180 g (6 oz) broccoli
salt and freshly ground black pepper
20 ml (4 tsp) butter
5-10 ml (1-2 tsp) chopped parsley

To Garnish:
herb sprigs

1 Finely shred or grate the courgettes, carrot and parsnip (keeping them separate). Divide the broccoli into small florets. Season each of the vegetables with salt and pepper.

2 Place 5 ml (1 tsp) butter in the bottom of each of 4 ramekins and sprinkle with the chopped parsley. Arrange the broccoli florets on top of and around the butter. Cover with the courgettes, followed by the carrot and finally the parsnip.

3 Cover each ramekin with foil, place in a steamer over boiling water and steam for approximately 5 minutes until just tender. (Alternatively cover the ramekins with cling film and microwave on high for about 1½ minutes.)

4 To serve, uncover the ramekins and invert onto warmed serving plates. Turn the vegetable crowns the right way up and garnish with herbs. Serve at once.

Note: The vegetable crowns will hold their shape once turned out.

Cheese and Sesame Tuile filled with Baby Vegetables

These very delicate savoury biscuits are rolled into cones and filled with steamed tiny vegetables.

Tuiles:
30 ml (2 tbsp) grated red Leicester cheese
15 ml (1 tbsp) softened butter
35 ml (2½ tbsp) plain flour
2.5 ml (½ tsp) paprika
1.25 ml (¼ tsp) cayenne pepper
large pinch of salt
30 ml (2 tbsp) milk (approximately), to mix
35 ml (2½ tbsp) sesame seeds

Vegetable Filling:
8-12 baby carrots
4-8 baby leeks
4-8 baby parsnips
12 green beans
tiny herb sprigs (eg parsley, dill)

1 To make the tuiles, beat the cheese and butter together in a bowl until evenly mixed. Add the flour, paprika, cayenne and salt, then mix in enough milk to make a soft dough. Stir in the sesame seeds.

2 Spread 4 thin rounds of the mixture, about 12 cm (5 inches) in diameter, on a baking sheet lined with non-stick baking parchment. Bake in a preheated oven at 200°C (400°F) mark 6 for 10-12 minutes until the edges are lightly browned.

3 Leave to cool for a minute or two on the baking sheet then, while still warm and pliable, shape around cream horn cones and leave to cool.

4 Steam the baby vegetables until just tender. Fill the tuiles with the hot vegetables, adding a few herb sprigs. Serve at once.

Caramelised Shallots

16 shallots or button onions, peeled
150 ml (¼ pint) lamb stock
25 g (1 oz) unsalted butter
25 g (1 oz) caster sugar
salt and freshly ground black pepper

1 Put the shallots into a heavy-based pan and cover with the stock. Bring to the boil, lower the heat and simmer for 10 minutes; drain well.

2 Melt the butter in the clean, dry pan, then add the shallots, sugar and seasoning. Cover and cook, stirring occasionally, for about 10 minutes until tender and glazed. Keep warm.

Caramelised Shallots and Garlic

20 shallots
16 cloves garlic
45 ml (3 tbsp) butter
salt and freshly ground black pepper
10 ml (2 tsp) sugar

1 Plunge the shallots into a pan of boiling water for 1 minute, then remove and, when cool enough to handle, peel away the skins (see note).

2 Place the shallots in a small ovenproof dish and add 30 ml (2 tbsp) butter. Season with salt and pepper, and sprinkle with half of the sugar. Cook in a preheated oven at 190°C (375°F) mark 5 for approximately 40 minutes until soft.

3 Meanwhile, place the unpeeled garlic cloves in another small ovenproof dish. Add the remaining 15 ml (1 tbsp) butter, seasoning and remaining sugar. Cover and cook in the oven (with the shallots) for about 30 minutes until soft. Snip the tips off the garlic and squeeze the cloves out of their skins to serve, with the shallots.

Note: For an attractive finish, remove the outer 1 or 2 layers from the shallots until they split into 2 halves.

Aubergine Crisps

oil for deep-frying
1 aubergine
salt and freshly ground black pepper

1 Heat the oil in a deep-fat fryer to 160°C (325°F).

2 Meanwhile, cut the aubergine into very fine slices and pat dry on kitchen paper.

3 Deep-fry the aubergine slices in the hot oil in small batches until crisp and golden; remove and drain on kitchen paper. Keep hot while frying the remainder. Season with salt and pepper to taste. Serve at once.

Beetroot and Preserved Lime Salad

4 smallish beetroot, freshly boiled and peeled
2 preserved lime quarters (see below), plus a little of the oil
2 spring onions, trimmed and chopped
5 ml (1 tsp) ground cumin
30 ml (2 tbsp) freshly chopped parsley
scant 15 ml (1 tbsp) olive oil
5 ml (1 tsp) caster sugar
10 ml (1 tsp) raspberry vinegar
freshly ground black pepper

1 Cut the beetroot into cubes and finely slice the preserved lime quarters.

2 Mix all the other ingredients together in a bowl. Add the beetroot and lime slices, toss to mix and set aside to allow the flavours to develop for 1 hour before serving.

Preserved Limes: To prepare these, scrub 500 g (1¼ lb) limes, then cut into quarters and put into a colander. Sprinkle generously with sea salt, and leave for at least 24 hours to soften. Pack the limes into a sterilised pickling jar. Add 4 dried red chillies, then add sufficient corn oil to cover. Seal tightly and set aside in a cool place for about 3 weeks. (Note that lemons and kumquats can be preserved in the same way.)

Butternut Squash Balls

45 ml (3 tbsp) olive oil
15 ml (1 tbsp) dried sage
1 large clove garlic, crushed
1 large butternut squash

1 Put the olive oil in a small bowl, add the sage and garlic and set aside to infuse.

2 Cut the squash in half lengthwise. Scoop out and discard the seeds. Using a melon baller, scoop out the flesh into balls, shaping as many as possible.

3 Put the squash balls in an ovenproof dish, add the oil mixture and turn to coat. Bake in a preheated oven at 180°C (350°F) mark 4 for 35 minutes or until tender.

Glazed Radishes

20 radishes, trimmed
15 ml (1 tbsp) butter
5 ml (1 tsp) sugar
salt and freshly ground black pepper

1 Place the radishes in a small pan with the butter, sugar and seasoning. Add enough water to barely cover them and bring to the boil.

2 Simmer gently, uncovered, until the radishes are cooked but still retain some bite, and the liquid has reduced down to a shiny glaze.

Root Vegetable Purée

225 g (8 oz) peeled parsnips
225 g (8 oz) peeled celeriac
225 g (8 oz) peeled carrots
large knob of butter
salt and freshly ground black pepper

1 Cook the vegetables in boiling salted water until tender. Drain, then work to a purée, using a food mill or masher.

2 Return to a low heat and heat through. Add the butter and season well to serve.

Parsnip Crisps

1 large parsnip (or 2 small ones)
oil for shallow-frying

1 Peel the parsnip(s) and cut in half across the middle. Pare into very thin slices, using a swivel vegetable peeler, avoiding the 'woody' centre.

2 Heat about a 2.5 cm (1 inch) depth of oil in a heavy-based deep frying pan and fry the parsnip slices in batches until crisp and golden brown. Drain on kitchen paper and keep warm until ready to serve. (They will stay crisp for up to 1 hour.)

Parsnip Purée with Parmesan

450 g (1 lb) parsnips, roughly chopped
salt and freshly ground black pepper
90 ml (3 fl oz) single cream
75 g (3 oz) Parmesan cheese, freshly grated
50 g (2 oz) butter

1 Cook the parsnips in boiling salted water for about 10 minutes until soft.

2 Drain the parsnips and place in a food processor. Add the cream, Parmesan, butter and seasoning. Process until smooth.

3 Transfer to a warmed ovenproof serving dish. Keep warm in the oven until ready to serve if necessary.

Puréed Parsnip Timbales

4 small parsnips, peeled, cored and diced
60 ml (4 tbsp) double cream
salt and freshly ground white pepper
8 large outer Savoy cabbage leaves
  (approximately)

1 Cook the parsnips in boiling salted water until soft, then drain. Purée the parsnips, using a hand-held blender or masher. Add the cream and seasoning; mix thoroughly.

2 Blanch the cabbage leaves in a large pan of boiling water for 10 seconds to set the colour. Drain thoroughly.

3 Line 4 buttered dariole moulds with the cabbage leaves and fill with the puréed parsnip mixture. Cover tightly with foil and place in a steamer over boiling water. Cook for 5 minutes, then turn the timbales out of the dariole moulds to serve.

Roast Parsnip 'Cups' filled with Parsnip Purée

7 medium parsnips
30-45 ml (2-3 tbsp) groundnut oil
salt and freshly ground black pepper
15 ml (1 tbsp) double cream
5 ml (1 tsp) butter
freshly grated nutmeg

1 Cut 2 rounds from each of 6 parsnips, about 3 cm (1¼ inches) in diameter and 1 cm (½ inch) deep, reserving the remaining pieces. Peel the parsnip rounds then, using the end of a potato peeler, hollow out the centres (without cutting right through) to form little cups.

2 Heat the oil in a roasting tin. Add the parsnips and baste with the oil, then put into a preheated oven at 180°C (350°F) mark 4. Cook for about 40 minutes, until tender, turning once halfway through cooking.

3 Meanwhile, peel the remaining parsnip and reserved pieces. Remove the hard core and cut into even-sized chunks. Cook in boiling salted water until soft. Drain thoroughly and mash with the cream, butter, and pepper and nutmeg to taste. Check the seasoning. Pass through a sieve, pressing the purée through with the back of a wooden spoon; set aside.

4 Drain the roast parsnip cups of any oil, then place a spoonful of parsnip purée in each one. Return to the oven for about 5 minutes, to warm through.

Note: If prepared in advance and cooled, you will need to warm these through in the oven for 8-10 minutes.

Horseradish Bubble and Squeak

125 g (4 oz) Brussels sprouts
125 g (4 oz) cabbage
65 g (2½ oz) unsalted butter
1 large onion, thinly sliced
1 clove garlic, crushed
450 g (1 lb) cooked potato
salt and freshly ground black pepper
7.5 ml (1½ tsp) grated fresh horseradish or
* 15 ml (1 tbsp) horseradish cream*

1 Cook the Brussels sprouts and cabbage in boiling salted water until tender; drain well.

2 Meanwhile, melt 15 g (½ oz) butter in a pan, add the onion and garlic, and cook gently for 4-5 minutes until softened.

3 Mash the potato, cabbage and sprouts together in a bowl, then add the onion and mix to a firm texture. Season with salt and pepper and add the horseradish.

4 Divide the mixture between four 10 cm (4 inch) pastry cutters, pressing well down. Melt the remaining butter in a large frying pan. Carefully transfer the cutters to the frying pan and cook for 4-5 minutes. Remove the cutters and transfer the bubble and squeak cakes to a preheated grill. Cook until golden brown on top. Serve piping hot.

Potato and Parsnip Rösti

300 g (10 oz) potatoes
300 g (10 oz) parsnips
salt and freshly ground black pepper
75 g (3 oz) unsalted butter

1 Place the unpeeled potatoes and parsnips in a pan of lightly salted water. Bring to the boil, lower the heat and simmer for 7-8 minutes.

2 Drain the potatoes and parsnips, then peel.

3 Grate them into a large bowl, avoiding the woody cores of the parsnips. Season with salt and pepper. Mix together, using your hands.

4 Divide the mixture into 4 portions and shape into cakes, approximately 9 cm (3½ inches) in diameter and 5 mm (¼ inch) thick.

5 Heat a quarter of the butter in a non-stick sauté pan. Add one of the rösti and sauté over a high heat for approximately 5 minutes each side until golden brown. During cooking, press down the rösti with the back of a small fish slice. Transfer to a warmed baking tray and keep warm in a low oven while cooking the remainder.

6 Serve piping hot, within 5-10 minutes of cooking the last rösti.

Note: If preferred, you can cook the rösti together in a large sauté pan.

Parsley Potatoes

5 medium potatoes
30 ml (2 tbsp) goose fat or butter
1 plump clove garlic, finely chopped
4 shallots, peeled
salt and freshly ground black pepper
45-60 ml (3-4 tbsp) chopped parsley

1 Peel the potatoes and cut into 1 cm (¾ inch) cubes. Rinse under cold running water and pat dry with a tea towel.

2 Heat the goose fat or butter in a sauté pan and add the potatoes. Cook over a high heat until they start to colour.

3 Add the garlic, shallots, and seasoning. Lower the heat and cook, uncovered, for about 30 minutes, until tender. Towards the end of the cooking time, add the chopped parsley, reserving a little for garnish.

4 Transfer to a warmed serving dish and sprinkle with the reserved parsley to serve.

Potato and Courgette Soufflés

1 courgette
225 g (8 oz) cooked peeled potato
40 g (1½ oz) butter
150 ml (¼ pint) water
35 g (1¼ oz) plain flour
1 egg, beaten
salt and freshly ground black pepper
oil for deep-frying

1 Grate the courgette, then press between two sheets of kitchen paper to absorb as much moisture as possible.

2 Meanwhile, mash the cooked potato with a third of the butter. Heat the remaining butter in a saucepan with the water until the butter has melted and the liquid is almost boiling. Remove the pan from the heat, immediately add the flour and beat into the liquid. Gradually add the egg, beating to form a glossy, elastic paste. Stir in the courgette and mashed potato, and season with salt and pepper to taste.

3 Transfer the mixture to a piping bag fitted with a large plain nozzle. Pipe small balls of the mixture onto a sheet of greaseproof paper.

4 Heat the oil in a deep-fat fryer to 190°C (375°F). Cook the potato and courgette balls in batches of up to six at a time. Gently slide them into the hot oil and cook for 4-5 minutes until puffed up and golden. Drain on kitchen paper and keep hot while cooking the remainder. Serve immediately.

Potato and Wild Mushroom Cake

60 g (2 oz) butter
750 g (1½-1¾ lb) old potatoes, peeled and thinly sliced
185 g (6 oz) mixed wild mushrooms, sliced (see note)
salt and freshly ground black pepper
freshly grated nutmeg
90 ml (3 fl oz) thick double cream

To Garnish:
herb sprigs

1 Line a loose-bottomed 20-23 cm (8-9 inch) cake tin with foil, then grease it with a little of the butter.

2 Layer the potato and mushroom slices in the tin, seasoning each layer with salt, pepper and nutmeg. Dot each layer with butter. Finish with a layer of potato slices.

3 Pour over the cream, cover with foil and bake in a preheated oven at 190°C (375°F) mark 5 for 1 hour. Remove the foil and bake for a further 30 minutes until the top is crisp and golden brown. Garnish with herbs to serve.

Note: If wild mushrooms are unavailable, cultivated varieties can be used. However, large flat mushrooms will discolour the potatoes.

Sautéed Potatoes

8 small potatoes
50 g (2 oz) clarified butter
salt and freshly ground black pepper

1 Peel and finely slice the potatoes, immersing them in a bowl of cold water as you do so, to prevent discolouration. Rinse well and pat dry on a clean tea-towel.

2 Heat the clarified butter in a large heavy-based frying pan. Add the potatoes and cook for 20-30 minutes, shaking the pan from time to time to ensure they cook evenly. The cooked potatoes should be slightly crisp. Season with salt and pepper to taste during cooking.

3 Arrange a mound of sautéed potatoes on each warmed serving plate to serve.

Note: Once cooked the potatoes can be kept warm in a preheated oven at 150°C (300°F) mark 2 until ready to serve.

Crispy Potatoes

3 medium potatoes, peeled and thinly sliced
salt and freshly ground black pepper
15 ml (1 tbsp) butter

1 Lay the potato slices in a buttered shallow ovenproof dish, overlapping them slightly. Season with salt and pepper.

2 Dot the butter over the potato slices and cook in a preheated oven at 180°C (350°F) mark 4 for about 40 minutes or until golden brown and cooked through. Serve piping hot.

Potatoes Lyonnaise

900 g (2 lb) waxy potatoes
200 g (7 oz) Gruyère cheese, grated
1½ cloves garlic, finely chopped
salt and freshly ground black pepper
600 ml (1 pint) double cream

1 Peel and thinly slice the potatoes and pat dry with kitchen paper. Layer the potatoes in a large well-buttered gratin dish, sprinkling each layer with the cheese, garlic and seasoning.

2 Heat the cream until almost boiling, then pour over the potatoes. Bake in a preheated oven at 190°C (375°F) for about 1½ hours until the potatoes are tender. If the top browns too quickly during baking, cover with foil.

Potatoes Dauphinois

6 medium-large potatoes (preferably a waxy variety), peeled
400 ml (14 fl oz) double cream
2.5 ml (½ tsp) salt
2 cloves garlic, crushed

1 Thinly slice the potatoes, rinse in cold water, drain and dry thoroughly. Layer the potatoes in a well-buttered 23 cm (9 inch) gratin dish.

2 Meanwhile, put the cream, salt and garlic in a pan. Heat until nearly boiling, stir well, then pour over the potatoes.

3 Cover the dish with foil and cook in a preheated oven at 180°C (350°F) mark 4 for about 1¼-1½ hours, removing the foil for the last 20 minutes to brown the top. Serve piping hot.

Individual Potatoes Dauphinois

450 g (1 lb) small potatoes
300 ml (½ pint) milk
5 ml (1 tsp) plain flour
150 ml (¼ pint) double cream
3 cloves garlic, crushed
salt and freshly ground black pepper

1 Peel and thinly slice the potatoes, then arrange overlapping in four 7.5 cm (3 inch) ramekins.

2 Put the milk in a saucepan. Mix the flour with a little of the cream to a smooth paste, then stir in the remaining cream. Add to the milk with the garlic and plenty of seasoning. Heat to boiling, then pour over the potatoes.

3 Cook in a preheated oven at 170°C (325°F) mark 3 for about 30 minutes, then increase the oven temperature to 200°C (400°F) mark 6 and bake for a further 10 minutes or until the tops are browned and the potatoes are tender. Serve piping hot.

Parmesan Puff Potatoes

550 g (1¼ lb) potatoes, peeled
salt and freshly ground black pepper
2 eggs (1 separated)
60 ml (4 tbsp) single cream
50 g (2 oz) butter
100 g (3½ oz) Parmesan cheese, freshly
  grated

1 Cook the potatoes in boiling salted water for 20 minutes or until tender. Drain and transfer the cooked potatoes to a food processor. Add the whole egg, egg yolk, cream, butter and 75 g (3 oz) of the Parmesan. Season with salt and pepper. Process briefly until evenly combined. Leave to cool slightly.

2 Grease 4 ramekins and sprinkle with the rest of the Parmesan. Whisk the egg white in a large bowl until it forms soft peaks, then carefully fold into the potato mixture. Divide equally between the ramekins.

3 Run a knife around the edge of each dish. Bake in a preheated oven at 200°C (400°F) mark 6 for 20 minutes or until risen and golden brown. Serve at once.

Horseradish Potatoes

1 garlic clove, halved
3 medium potatoes
90 ml (3 fl oz) double cream
60 ml (2 fl oz) milk
20 ml (1½ tbsp) creamed horseradish
salt and freshly ground black pepper
15 ml (1 tbsp) butter, in pieces

1 Rub an ovenproof dish with the cut garlic clove. Finely slice the potatoes and soak in a bowl of cold water to remove excess starch.

2 Put the double cream and milk in a saucepan and bring to the boil. Allow to cool slightly, then add the creamed horseradish and season with salt and pepper.

3 Drain the potatoes and pat dry. Arrange the potato slices in neat, even layers in the ovenproof dish, pouring a little of the cream mixture over each layer. Pour the remaining cream mixture on top and dot with the butter. Bake in a preheated oven at 180°C (350°F) mark 4 for about 40 minutes or until cooked through and golden brown on top.

Stoved New Potatoes

16-20 new potatoes, depending on size
30 ml (2 tbsp) water
salt and freshly ground black pepper
40 g (1½ oz) unsalted butter, diced

1 Peel the potatoes and place in a single layer in a heavy-based pan (one which has a tight-fitting lid). Add the water and seasoning. Dot the butter onto the potatoes.

2 Cover the pan with a double layer of foil, then position the lid to ensure a very tight fit. Cook over a very low heat for 45 minutes to 1 hour, until tender, shaking the pan from time to time to prevent the potatoes sticking.

Saffron Mash

Saffron imparts a wonderful yellow tone to creamy mashed potato in this simple accompaniment.

300 g (10 oz) potatoes, peeled
salt and freshly ground black pepper
pinch of saffron strands
30 ml (2 tbsp) butter
45 ml (3 tbsp) crème fraîche

1 Cook the potatoes in boiling salted water with the saffron added until tender.

2 Drain the potatoes and mash with the butter and crème fraîche. Season with salt and pepper to taste. Serve at once.

Creamed Potatoes with Truffle

700 g (1½ lb) King Edward potatoes
150 ml (¼ pint) single cream
   (approximately)
salt
1 small bottled black truffle, drained and
   finely chopped

1 Prick the potato skins with a fork, then bake in a preheated oven at 200°C (400°F) mark 6 for 1½ hours.

2 Halve the potatoes and scoop out the flesh from the skins into a heatproof bowl. Mash well and beat in sufficient cream to give a smooth, yet still quite stiff consistency. Season lightly with salt, then carefully stir in the truffle. Cover and return to a warm oven to heat through.

Anna Potatoes

700 g (1½ lb) potatoes
salt and freshly ground black pepper
25 g (1 oz) butter

1 Peel and thinly slice the potatoes. Layer in a greased ovenproof dish, seasoning each layer with salt and pepper.

2 Dot with butter, cover with foil and bake in a preheated oven at 190°C (375°F) mark 5 for 1 hour.

3 Remove from the oven and leave to stand for 5 minutes before serving.

Potato Galettes

250 g (9 oz) potatoes, peeled
salt and freshly ground black pepper
75 g (3 oz) butter, melted

1 Finely grate the potatoes, season with salt and pepper and mix with the melted butter. Position a 7.5 cm (3 inch) metal pastry cutter on a greased baking tray and fill with the potato mixture to a depth of 5 mm (¼ inch), pressing well down. Carefully remove the metal ring and repeat with the remaining mixture.

2 Bake in a preheated oven at 200°C (400°C) mark 6 for 10 minutes. Turn the potato galettes over and bake for a further 10 minutes or until golden and cook through. Serve hot.

Baby Potato Kebabs

12 baby new potatoes
4 cloves garlic, peeled
4 large shallots, peeled
mint-flavoured olive oil, for basting (see note)
coarse sea salt

1 Presoak 4 wooden kebab skewers in cold water (to prevent scorching during grilling). Place the potatoes in their skins in a steamer and steam over boiling water. After 5 minutes, add the whole garlic cloves and shallots to the steamer. Steam for a further 2-3 minutes until the potatoes, garlic and shallots are starting to soften. Remove and leave until cool enough to handle.

2 Halve the shallots. Peel the potatoes and take off a small slice from each potato so it will lie flat. Thread the kebab ingredients alternately onto the 4 wooden skewers in the following order: potato, shallot half, garlic clove, potato, shallot half, potato.

3 Place the kebabs on a baking or roasting sheet. brush liberally with the minted oil and sprinkle with salt. Place under a preheated grill and cook, turning occasionally, for 4-5 minutes or until starting to brown. Serve hot.

Note: To prepare the mint-flavoured oil, immerse sprigs of fresh mint in olive oil and leave to infuse for a few days.

Mejadarra with Mushrooms

2 large mild onions, halved lengthwise
10-15 ml (2-3 tsp) vegetable oil
2.5 ml (½ tsp) ground turmeric
5-10 ml (1-2 tsp) freshly ground cumin seeds
5-10 ml (1-2 tsp) freshly ground coriander
   seeds
100 g (3½ oz) large green lentils, soaked in
   cold water for 2-3 hours
300 ml (½ pint) beef or chicken stock
150 g (5 oz) basmati rice
salt and freshly ground black pepper
30 ml (2 tbsp) grapeseed oil (approximately)
10-12 chestnut mushrooms, sliced
handful of fresh coriander sprigs, roughly
   chopped

1 Finely chop one of the onion halves. Heat the vegetable oil in a pan, add the chopped onion and fry gently until softened. Add the spices and stir well. Drain the lentils and add to the pan with the stock. Bring to the boil, cover and simmer for about 20 minutes until the lentils are soft.

2 Meanwhile, put the rice in a small saucepan, cover with cold water and bring to the boil. Stir once, then lower the heat and cook for 3 minutes. Drain and rinse with cold water.

3 When the lentils are soft, add the par-boiled rice. Stir well. (Add a little water to cover if necessary.) Add salt to taste and a generous sprinkling of pepper. Bring to the boil, lower the heat, cover and cook until the liquid is absorbed and the rice is cooked.

4 Meanwhile, slice the remaining onion halves into crescent shapes. Heat the grapeseed oil in a frying pan, add the onions and fry over a medium heat until almost caramelised. Drain on kitchen paper and keep warm in the oven. Add the mushrooms to the pan, with a little more oil if necessary, and fry until tender and browned. Drain and keep warm with the onions. Stir-fry half of the coriander briefly in the remaining oil.

5 Add the rest of the coriander to the mejadarra and fork it through. Divide between warmed serving plates and top with the fried onions. Garnish with the mushrooms and fried coriander to serve.

Parsley Rice

200 g (7 oz) long-grain rice
15 g (½ oz) butter
30 ml (2 tbsp) finely chopped parsley
salt and freshly ground black pepper

1 Rinse the rice thoroughly in several changes of cold water until the water becomes clear.

2 Put the rice into a saucepan and add 400 ml (14 fl oz) water. Bring to the boil, lower the heat and simmer gently for about 15-20 minutes until the water is absorbed. Turn off the heat and leave to stand for about 15 minutes. (If using an electric rice cooker, cook according to the manufacturer's directions.)

3 Meanwhile, melt the butter in a frying pan, add the parsley with salt and pepper to taste and fry gently for 2-3 minutes.

4 Fluff up the rice, add the fried parsley and toss well.

5 Put a quarter of the rice into a warmed buttered dariole mould or cup. Press down, then turn out onto a warmed serving plate. Repeat with the other portions. Serve immediately.

Creamed Polenta

1 small onion, finely chopped
1 clove garlic, crushed
600 ml (1 pint) milk
300 ml (½ pint) single cream
60 ml (4 tbsp) chopped chives
60 ml (4 tbsp) chopped parsley
175 g (6 oz) quick-cook (instant) polenta
salt and freshly ground black pepper

1 Put the onion, garlic, milk and cream in a saucepan and bring to the boil. Simmer gently until the onion is soft.

2 Add the herbs, then shower in the polenta in a steady stream, stirring constantly. Beat until smooth. Cook over a low heat, stirring continuously, for 5 minutes. Season with salt and pepper to taste. Serve at once.

Desserts

Pear and Almond Mille Feuille

80 g (3¼ oz) unsalted butter
80 g (3¼ oz) flaked almonds, toasted
90 g (3½ oz) icing sugar
1 egg (size 2)
15 ml (1 tbsp) dark rum
6 sheets of filo pastry
melted butter, for brushing
120 ml (4 fl oz) double cream
15 ml (1 tbsp) caster sugar
125 g (4 oz) mascarpone
15 ml (1 tbsp) poire William liqueur
2 ripe pears
icing sugar, for dusting

To Serve:
120 ml (4 fl oz) single cream
raspberry coulis (optional)

1 Cream the butter in a heatproof bowl until softened, then add the almonds, icing sugar and egg. Stand the bowl over a pan of simmering water and stir gently until the butter has melted and the mixture is slightly thickened. Stir in the rum, then allow to cool. Chill in the refrigerator until needed.

2 Brush the sheets of filo pastry generously with melted butter, then fold each sheet into a long strip, about 4 cm (1½ inches) wide. Cut twelve 10 cm (4 inch) lengths in total. Brush with melted butter and place on a baking sheet. Bake in a preheated oven at 200°C (400°F) mark 6 for 5-10 minutes until golden and crisp. Transfer to a wire rack to cool.

3 Whip the cream and sugar together in a bowl until it forms soft peaks. Briefly whip the mascarpone, then fold into the cream with the poire William liqueur.

4 Peel, core and slice the pears. Fold into the cream mixture.

5 Place one filo wafer in the centre of each serving plate. Cover with the chilled nut paste, then place another filo wafer on top. Cover with the cream and pear mixture, then top with the remaining filo wafers. Dust with icing sugar. Serve immediately, on a pool of cream, surrounded by a raspberry coulis if desired.

Individual Grape Tarts with Almond Crème Patissière and a Fruit Coulis

Sweetcrust Pastry:
200 g (7 oz) plain flour
40 g (1½ oz) ground almonds
120 g (4 oz) icing sugar
pinch of salt
100 g (3½ oz) butter, in small pieces
½ egg (approximately), beaten

Filling:
250 ml (8 fl oz) milk
3 egg yolks (size 2)
15 ml (1 tbsp) icing sugar
25 g (1 oz) cornflour
50 g (2 oz) ground almonds
25 g (1 oz) butter, in small pieces
400 g (14 oz) seedless black grapes, halved
400 g (14 oz) seedless white grapes, halved

Fruit Coulis:
about 225 g (8 oz) mixed red fruit (eg
   strawberries, raspberries and redcurrants)
about 25 g (1 oz) sugar, to taste
squeeze of lemon juice

To Finish:
icing sugar, for dusting

1 To make the pastry, put the flour, ground almonds, icing sugar and salt into a food processor. Add the butter and process briefly until the mixture resembles fine crumbs. Add sufficient egg to bind the mixture and form a soft dough. Wrap in cling film and leave to rest in the refrigerator for 30 minutes.

2 To make the crème patissière, pour the milk into a saucepan and bring almost to the boil. Meanwhile, beat the egg yolks and icing sugar together in a bowl until very pale in colour, then beat in the cornflour, until smooth. Gradually add the milk, whisking constantly. Return to the pan and cook over a low heat, stirring constantly with a wooden spoon, until thickened. Take off the heat, then stir in the ground almonds and butter.

3 Roll out the pastry thinly on a lightly floured surface and use to line four 10 cm (4 inch) individual flan tins. Prick the bases with a fork, line with greaseproof paper and baking beans and bake blind in a pre-heated oven at 190°C (375°F) mark 5 for 15 minutes. Let cool slightly, then remove the beans and paper and allow to cool.

4 Arrange the grape halves in the flan cases, alternating the colours to form a pattern. Pour over the crème patissière, position 3 grape halves in the centre and bake in the oven for 20 minutes.

5 Meanwhile, prepare the coulis. Place the fruits in a saucepan and cook gently until softened. Sweeten with sugar to taste. Pass through a nylon sieve into a bowl to remove the pips, then add a squeeze of lemon juice to taste.

6 Allow the tarts to cool slightly, then place on individual serving plates and dust with icing sugar. Serve with the coulis.

Quince Tart with Vulscombe Cheese Mousse and Figs in Rosewater Syrup

If possible, prepare the syrup for the figs a day in advance to allow the flavours to infuse.

Figs in Rosewater Syrup:
225 g (8 oz) caster sugar
600 ml (1 pint) water
1 orange, quartered
1 lemon, quartered
1 cinnamon stick
4 figs
60 ml (4 tbsp) rosewater

Quince Tart:
125 g (4 oz) unsalted butter, at room
  temperature
50 g (2 oz) icing sugar, sifted
finely grated rind of 1 lemon
2 egg yolks
175 g (6 oz) plain flour, sifted
175 g (6 oz) quince cheese

Vulscombe Mousse:
3 gelatine leaves
60 ml (4 tbsp) milk
1 vulscombe or other full-fat soft goat's
  cheese, about 175 g (6 oz)
175 g (6 oz) fromage frais
15 ml (1 tbsp) icing sugar
2 egg whites

1 First make the syrup for the figs. Put the sugar and water in a saucepan over a low heat until the sugar is dissolved. Add the orange and lemon quarters, together with the cinnamon stick. Bring the syrup to the boil, then remove from the heat and leave to cool, overnight if possible. Strain the syrup and set aside.

2 To make the pastry for the tart, put the butter and icing sugar into a food processor and work until pale and fluffy. Add the lemon rind and egg yolks and process until evenly blended. Add the flour and work until just amalgamated; the dough will form a ball and leave the sides of the bowl. Wrap the dough in cling film and leave to rest in the refrigerator for at least 1 hour.

3 To prepare the mousse, soak the gelatine leaves in cold water to cover. Meanwhile warm the milk. Squeeze out excess water from the gelatine, then add to the milk and stir until dissolved. Put the cheese and fromage frais into a food processor and blend until smooth and creamy. Add the icing sugar, then with the motor running, add the dissolved gelatine mixture through the feeder tube and process briefly. Whisk the egg whites in a separate bowl until they form soft peaks, then fold in the cheese mixture.

4 Spoon the mixture into 4 ramekins, cover loosely with cling film and chill in the refrigerator for 1 hour or until set.

5 Roll out the pastry to just under a 5 mm (¼ inch) thickness and cut four 7.5 cm (3 inch) rounds. Transfer to a baking tray, prick with a fork, and let rest in the refrigerator for 20 minutes. (Freeze the remaining pastry for another occasion.)

6 Bake the pastry rounds in a preheated oven at 180°C (350°F) mark 4 for 5-7 minutes until pale golden. Transfer to a wire rack to cool.

7 To cook the figs, put 300 ml (½ pint) of the syrup in a pan with the rosewater. Bring to a simmer, add the figs and poach gently for 15-20 minutes. Remove the figs with a slotted spoon; boil the syrup to reduce by half. Let cool.

8 Cut the quince cheese into 3 mm (⅛ inch) slices, then cut out circles about 2 cm (¾ inch) in diameter; halve each circle. Arrange the quince slices, overlapping, on the pastry circles, to cover them completely.

9 To serve the dessert, spread a pool of the rose-coloured syrup on each serving plate. Turn out the mousses and position one on each plate, with a fig and a portion of quince tart.

Note: Jars of quince cheese are available from delicatessens, but if you have a quince tree you can, of course, make your own. Sweeten 600 ml (1 pint) quince pulp with 450 g (1 lb) sugar, boil until thickened, then set in sterilised jars.

Treacle Tart with Lemon Zest and Custard Sauce

Pastry:
175 g (6 oz) plain flour
125 g (4 oz) unsalted butter, in pieces
few drops of milk (if required)

Filling:
125 g (4 oz) fresh white breadcrumbs
finely grated zest and juice of 1 lemon
10 rounded tbsp golden syrup
2 rounded tbsp black treacle

Custard Sauce:
300 ml (½ pint) double cream
3 egg yolks
5 ml (1 tsp) cornflour
15 ml (1 tbsp) sugar
few drops of vanilla essence

1 To make the pastry, put the flour and butter into a food processor and work to a smooth dough; the mixture should start to form a ball without any additional liquid, but it may be necessary to add a few drops of milk to bind the pastry.

2 Divide the pastry into 4 portions and use to line four individual 10 cm (4 inch) flan tins. As the pastry is very short and quite difficult to roll, you will find it easier to press the pastry directly into the tins, rather than roll it out first.

3 For the filling, put the breadcrumbs, lemon rind, syrup and treacle in a bowl and mix until evenly blended.

4 Pour the filling into the flan cases and bake in a preheated oven at 180°C (350°F) mark 4 for 30-35 minutes until set. Leave to cool slightly in the tins before removing.

5 Meanwhile, make the custard sauce. Pour the cream into a heavy-based pan and bring just to boiling point. In the meantime, beat the egg yolks, cornflour, sugar and vanilla essence together in a bowl. Pour on the hot cream, whisking constantly. Return the custard to the pan and cook over a low heat for 1-2 minutes, stirring constantly with a wooden spoon until it is thick enough to coat the back of the spoon. Do not allow to boil or it will curdle.

6 Place the treacle tarts on individual plates and serve with the custard sauce.

Note: To make it easier to measure out the syrup, first warm the tablespoon.

Pear and Almond Tart with Amaretto Ice Cream

Ice Cream:
150 ml (¼ pint) milk
2 egg yolks
110 g (4 oz) caster sugar
150 ml (¼ pint) double cream
30 ml (2 tbsp) Amaretto liqueur

Pastry:
1 egg yolk
15 ml (1 tbsp) whipping cream
40 g (1½ oz) icing sugar
few drops of vanilla essence
75 g (3 oz) unsalted butter, softened
110 g (4 oz) plain flour
15 g (½ oz) cornflour

Filling:
25 g (1 oz) unsalted butter
25 g (1 oz) icing sugar
25 g (1 oz) ground almonds
1 egg (size 3)
15 ml (1 tbsp) cream
1 ripe pear

Glaze:
50 g (2 oz) apricot jam, warmed and sieved

To Decorate:
redcurrants (or other seasonal fruit)
icing sugar, for dusting

1 To make the ice cream, pour the milk into a saucepan and slowly bring to the boil. Meanwhile, beat the egg yolks and sugar together in a bowl. Gradually pour on the milk, whisking constantly. Return the mixture to the pan and cook over a low heat, stirring constantly, until the custard begins to thicken; do not allow to boil or it will curdle. Leave until cold, then stir in the cream and Amaretto liqueur.

2 Transfer to an ice-cream maker and churn according to the manufacturer's directions. Alternatively freeze in a shallow container, whisking 2 or 3 times during freezing to break down the ice crystals and ensure an even-textured result.

3 To make the pastry, beat the egg yolk, whipping cream, icing sugar and vanilla essence together in a bowl. Mix in the softened butter. Sift in the flour and cornflour, stir well and form into a dough, using your hands, adding a little more flour to bind if necessary. Wrap in cling film and leave to rest in the refrigerator for 1 hour.

4 For the filling, mix the butter, icing sugar, ground almonds, egg and cream together in a bowl to form a smooth paste.

5 Divide the pastry into 4 portions and use to line four buttered 10 cm (4 inch) individual flan tins. (It will probably be necessary to do this with fingers as the pastry is too crumbly to roll.) Refrigerate for 10 minutes.

6 In the meantime, peel, quarter and core the pear. Slice lengthwise, leaving the stalk end intact, and fan out. Fill the pastry cases with the almond cream and lay the fanned pear quarters on top. Bake in a preheated oven at 190°C (375°F) mark 5 for 25-30 minutes.

7 Remove the tarts from the oven and while still warm brush with the warm apricot glaze. Carefully remove the tarts from their tins and place on plates. Spoon the amaretto ice cream onto the plates, and decorate with redcurrants or other fruit. Dust with icing sugar and serve at once.

Blackcurrant Tart with Lime Sorbet

Pastry:
150 g (5 oz) unsalted butter, diced
   (at room temperature)
90 g (3½ oz) icing sugar
1 egg (size 3), beaten
275 g (9 oz) plain flour

Filling:
350 g (12 oz) blackcurrants
5 ml (1 tsp) ground cinnamon
90 ml (6 tbsp) crème de cassis
60-90 ml (4-6 tbsp) soft brown sugar
2 eggs (size 1)
2 egg yolks (size 1)
250 ml (8 fl oz) whipping cream
60 ml (4 tbsp) demerara sugar
grated rind of 1 lime

Lime Sorbet:
10 limes
caster sugar (see recipe)
30 ml (2 tbsp) triple lime liquor

1 First make the pastry. Beat the butter and icing sugar together in a bowl until light and fluffy. Gradually beat in the egg. Sift in the flour and stir until the mixture comes together. Form the pastry into a ball, wrap in cling film and chill in the refrigerator, preferably overnight.

2 To make the lime sorbet, squeeze the juice from 8 limes and measure the volume of juice obtained; set aside. Measure an equal volume of caster sugar. Cut the remaining 2 limes into quarters and discard the pips. Place the lime quarters in a food processor with the sugar and process to a pulp. Add the reserved lime juice and lime liquor; process briefly. Transfer to an ice-cream machine and churn until frozen.

3 Roll out the chilled pastry as thinly as possible, and use to line an 18 cm (7 inch) loose-bottomed flan tin. Leave to rest in the refrigerator for 30 minutes. (Freeze the leftover pastry for another occasion.)

4 Line the pastry case with greaseproof paper and baking beans and bake blind in a preheated oven at 200°C (400°F) mark 6 for 10-15 minutes until firm, but not coloured. Remove the paper and beans.

5 Put the blackcurrants in a saucepan with the cinnamon and 30 ml (2 tbsp) of the crème de cassis. Sweeten to taste with the brown sugar, then turn into the part-baked pastry case.

6 In a bowl, beat together the whole eggs, egg yolks, whipping cream, demerara sugar, lime rind and remaining 60 ml (4 tbsp) crème de cassis. Pour over the black-currants in the pastry case.

7 Return the tart to the oven and bake for 15-20 minutes until the filling is just firm. Let stand for 5 minutes, then remove from the flan tin.

8 To serve, cut the tart into 4 portions and place on individual serving plates. Serve warm with a generous scoop of lime sorbet.

Note: If you do not have an ice-cream maker, freeze the sorbet in a shallow container, whisking 2 or 3 times during freezing to break down the ice crystals and ensure an even-textured result.

Lemon and Almond Tart with a Lemon Sabayon and Amaretto Cream

Pastry:
175 g (6 oz) plain flour
125 g (4 oz) butter
40 g (1½ oz) ground almonds
40 g (1½ oz) flaked almonds
10 ml (2 tsp) Amaretto liqueur
2.5 ml (½ tsp) almond essence
5-10 ml (1-2 tsp) cold water, to mix

Filling:
2 eggs
100 g (3½ oz) caster sugar
90 ml (6 tbsp) double cream
40 g (1½ oz) unsalted butter, melted and cooled
finely grated zest of 1 lemon
juice of 2-2½ lemons

Amaretto Cream:
150 ml (¼ pint) double cream
12.5 ml (2½ tsp) icing sugar, sifted
15 ml (1 tbsp) Amaretto liqueur

Lemon Sabayon:
2 egg yolks
25 ml (1½ tbsp) caster sugar
7.5 ml (1 ½ tsp) lemon juice
30 ml (2 tbsp) cold water

1 To make the pastry, sift the flour into a bowl and rub in the butter until the mixture resembles breadcrumbs. Stir in the ground and flaked almonds, then add the Amaretto liqueur, almond essence and 5 ml (1 tsp) cold water. Mix with a round-bladed knife, then use your fingers to bind the pastry together; adding a little more water if necessary.

2 Roll out the pastry and use to line a greased 20 cm (8 inch) flan tin. (As the pastry is very soft, almost like a paste, it may crack as you line the tin. Simply mould it together and the pastry will bake evenly.)

3 Prick the base and sides with a fork and line the flan case with greaseproof paper and baking beans. Bake blind near the top of the oven at 180°C (350°F) mark 4 for about 12 minutes, then remove the paper and beans and cook for a further 10 minutes, or until the pastry is golden brown. Lower the oven setting to 160°C (325°F) mark 3.

4 While the pastry is cooking, make the filling. Whisk the eggs and sugar together in a bowl until pale and thick, then stir in the cream and cooled melted butter. Mix well, then add the lemon zest and juice of 2-2½ lemons to taste.

5 Carefully pour the filling into the pastry case. (You may find it easiest to do this while the pastry case is in the oven – on the middle shelf where it needs to be moved to.) Bake for about 25 minutes until golden brown on top and firm to the touch.

6 Remove from the oven, let cool for about 30 minutes, then refrigerate for at least 1 hour before serving.

7 To make the Amaretto cream, put the cream, icing sugar and Amaretto liqueur in a bowl and whisk until it just starts to thicken. Refrigerate until needed.

8 To make the lemon sabayon, put all of the ingredients in a heatproof bowl and mix well, using a balloon whisk. Stand the bowl over a saucepan one-third full of simmering water, ensuring that the water doesn't touch the bowl. Whisk lightly until the mixture thickens, is a little frothy and pale cream colour. Immediately remove the bowl from the pan and pour the sabayon onto individual serving plates. Add a portion of lemon tart and a spoonful of amaretto cream. Serve at once.

Damson Tart with Meringue Topping

Pastry:
110 g (4 oz) unsalted butter
50 g (2 oz) icing sugar
1 egg yolk
110 g (4 oz) plain flour
25 g (1 oz) ground rice
pinch of salt

Filling:
450 g (1 lb) damsons
110 g (4 oz) caster sugar, or to taste
30 ml (2 tbsp) cornflour, blended with
*   30 ml (2 tbsp) water*
2 egg yolks (size 2), beaten

Meringue Topping:
3 egg whites (size 2)
75 g (3 oz) caster sugar

1 To make the pastry, cream together the butter and icing sugar in a bowl. Mix in the egg yolk until thoroughly incorporated. Add the flour and ground rice, together with the salt. Work in using your fingertips; the mixture should start to form a ball without any additional liquid. Wrap the pastry in cling film and chill in the refrigerator for at least 30 minutes.

2 For the filling, place the damsons in a heavy-based pan. Cover and cook over a low heat until the fruit is soft. Press through a nylon sieve into a bowl to remove the tough skins and stones. Stir in the sugar. Set aside about 60 ml (4 tbsp) of the damson purée for decoration.

3 Place the rest of the damson purée in a saucepan and reheat. Add the blended cornflour and bring to the boil, stirring constantly. Cook, stirring, for 1 minute until slightly thickened. Remove from the heat and allow to cool slightly, then beat in the egg yolks. Allow to cool.

4 Meanwhile, roll out the pastry thinly and use to line four individual 10 cm (4 inch) tartlet tins or one 23 cm (9 inch) tin. Line with greaseproof paper and baking beans and bake blind in a preheated oven at 160°C (325°F) mark 3 for 10 minutes. Remove the paper and beans and allow to cool slightly. Lower the oven temperature to 150°C (300°F) mark 2.

5 In the meantime, make the meringue topping. Whisk the egg whites in a bowl until they hold stiff peaks, then whisk in half of the sugar. Gradually fold in the rest of the sugar.

6 Spread a layer of damson purée in each pastry case, then cover with the meringue; do not overfill the tarts. Cook in the oven for 20 minutes. Allow to cool.

7 Serve cold with a swirl of damson purée, thinned if necessary with a little water.

Grapefruit Tart with Orange Sauce and Vanilla Cream

Pastry:
200 g (7 oz) plain flour
pinch of salt
25 g (1 oz) caster sugar
100 g (3½ oz) butter, in pieces
a little water, to bind

Filling:
50 g (2 oz) butter
50 ml (2 fl oz) grapefruit juice
50 g (2 oz) caster sugar
4 eggs, beaten

Decoration:
50 g (2 oz) butter
zest of 1 grapefruit
zest of 1 orange
zest of 1 lime

Sauce:
300 ml (½ pint) orange juice
150 g (5 oz) caster sugar
50 ml (2 fl oz) Grand Marnier or other
   orange liqueur
few drops of vanilla essence
200 ml (7 fl oz) double cream

1 To make the pastry, sift the flour, salt and sugar into a bowl. Rub in the butter until the mixture resembles fine crumbs. Add the minimum amount of cold water to bind the pastry and form a stiff dough. Wrap in cling film and leave to rest in the refrigerator for at least 30 minutes.

2 Roll out the pastry thinly and use to line four 10 cm (4 inch) individual flan tins. Line with greaseproof paper and baking beans and bake blind in a preheated oven at 200°C (400°F) mark 6 for 15-20 minutes. Remove the paper and beans. Cool on a wire rack.

3 To prepare the filling, melt the butter in a heatproof bowl over a pan of boiling water (or a double saucepan). Add the grapefruit juice and sugar and stir until dissolved. Add the eggs and whisk over the heat until the mixture thickens. Remove the bowl from the heat and allow to cool, stirring occasionally to prevent a skin forming.

4 For the decoration, heat the butter in a small pan, add the grapefruit, orange and lime zest and fry until crisp and lightly browned. Remove from the pan and drain on kitchen paper; set aside.

5 To make the sauce, put the orange juice and sugar in a saucepan and dissolve over a low heat. Increase the heat and cook steadily until the sauce is reduced by about half, and thickened. Allow to cool slightly, then add the liqueur. Add a few drops of vanilla essence to the cream, then stir into the sauce.

6 Divide the grapefruit filling between the pastry cases, spreading it evenly.

7 To serve, pour the orange sauce around one half of each serving plate, so that it coats a semi-circle. Pour the cream onto the other half of each plate. Place the tarts in the middle and decorate with a spoonful of the fried citrus zest.

Note: For the decoration, use a zester to remove the rinds from the citrus fruits in fine shreds.

Raspberry Tart with Vanilla Ice Cream

Pastry:
150 g (5 oz) unsalted butter (at room
temperature), diced
100 g (3½ oz) icing sugar
1 egg (size 3), beaten
250 g (9 oz) plain flour

Filling:
450 g (1 lb) raspberries
45 ml (3 tbsp) crème de framboise liqueur
icing sugar, to taste

Glaze:
90 ml (6 tbsp) good quality seedless
raspberry jam
juice of ¼ lemon

Vanilla Ice Cream:
2 vanilla pods
3 egg yolks
100 g (3½ oz) caster sugar
250 ml (8 fl oz) milk
300 ml (½ pint) double cream

1 To make the pastry, beat the butter and icing sugar together in a bowl, until light and fluffy. Gradually beat in the egg. Sift the flour into the bowl. Mix until the dough comes together. Form the pastry into a ball, wrap in cling film and chill in the refrigerator for at least 1 hour, preferably overnight.

2 To make the ice cream, split the vanilla pods and scrape the seeds out into a bowl, reserving the pods. Add the egg yolks and sugar and whisk until smooth. Pour the milk into a heavy-based saucepan and add the vanilla pods. Heat slowly until just below boiling point. Discard the vanilla pods, then pour the hot milk onto the egg and sugar mixture, whisking all the time.

3 Pour the custard back into the pan and stir constantly over a moderate heat until the mixture is just thick enough to lightly coat the back of a spoon; do not allow to boil or the custard will curdle. Remove from the heat and stir in the cream. Churn in an ice-cream maker until firm.

4 Roll out the chilled pastry as thinly as possible and use to line an 18 cm (7 inch) loose-bottomed flan tin. Leave to rest in the refrigerator for 30 minutes. (Freeze leftover pastry for another occasion.) Line the flan case with greaseproof paper and baking beans and bake blind in a preheated oven at 200°C (400°F) mark 6 for 10-15 minutes until firm, but not coloured.

5 Meanwhile, prepare the filling. Put the raspberries into a bowl with the crème de framboise. Stir gently to mix, adding icing sugar to taste. Leave to steep for 15 minutes. Remove the raspberries with a slotted spoon, reserving the juice, and use to fill the part-baked pastry shell. Return to the oven for a further 15-20 minutes or until the pastry is golden brown.

6 Meanwhile prepare the glaze. Put the jam and lemon juice in a small heavy-based pan with 30 ml (2 tbsp) of the reserved juice from the raspberries. Heat, stirring, until the jam is dissolved.

7 Remove the cooked tart from the oven and brush with the warm glaze.

8 To serve, cut the tart into 4 portions and place on individual serving plates. Serve warm with a scoop of vanilla ice cream.

Note: If you do not have an ice-cream maker, freeze the ice cream in a shallow container, whisking 2 or 3 times during freezing to break down the ice crystals and ensure an even-textured result.

Individual Apple Pies, with Cardamom Ice Cream and Crab Apple Sauce

Ice Cream:
10 cardamom pods
15 ml (1 tbsp) Bourbon whisky
30 ml (2 tbsp) granulated sugar
45 ml (3 tbsp) water
3 egg yolks
700 ml (½ pint) double cream

Almond Pastry:
200 g (7 oz) self-raising flour
pinch of salt
150 g (5 oz) butter, chilled and diced
50 g (2 oz) caster sugar
25 g (1 oz) chopped almonds
1 egg yolk
10 ml (2 tsp) iced water
2.5 ml (½ tsp) almond essence

Buttered Apple Filling:
700 g (1½ lb) well-flavoured firm dessert apples
50 g (2 oz) clarified butter
125 g (4 oz) sugar

Crab Apple Sauce:
4 poached crab apples home-preserved in syrup (see note)
5 ml (1 tsp) arrowroot, blended with a little water

To Decorate:
toasted almonds
icing sugar, for dusting

1 To make the ice cream, pound the cardamom pods in a mortar to release the flavour, then place in a small (lidded) container with the Bourbon. Cover and leave in a warm place to infuse for at least 2-3 hours, or longer if possible.

2 Put the sugar and water in a small pan and dissolve over a low heat. Increase the heat and boil until the syrup registers 110°C (230°F) on a sugar thermometer; ie the thread stage is reached.

3 Meanwhile, lightly whisk the egg yolks in a bowl. Gradually pour in the boiling syrup, whisking constantly. Continue whisking until the mixture is cool and very thick. Fold in the cream, then add the strained flavoured whisky to taste.

4 Transfer to an ice-cream maker and churn for 20 minutes, then turn into a freezerproof container and freeze until required. (If you do not have an ice-cream maker, freeze in a shallow container, whisking periodically during freezing to break down the ice crystals and ensure an even-textured result.)

5 To make the pastry, sift the flour and salt into a bowl. Add the butter and rub in lightly until the mixture resembles crumbs. Stir in the sugar and chopped almonds. Mix the egg yolk with the water and almond essence. Add to the dry ingredients and work to a smooth dough, using your fingertips. Gather up the dough, flour lightly and wrap in cling film. Chill in the refrigerator for at least 20 minutes or until needed.

6 Oil 4 individual 10 cm (4 inch) loose-bottomed flan tins. Divide two thirds of the pastry into 4 portions; keep the rest wrapped. Roll out one piece at a time on a lightly floured surface and use to line each flan tin. When you have lined all the tins, prick the bases with a fork, then line with a square of oiled foil and baking beans. Bake blind in a preheated oven at 190°C (375°F) mark 5 for 5-6 minutes. Remove the beans and foil, then bake for a further 3-5 minutes to cook the bases. Let cool slightly in the tins.

7 Meanwhile, roll out the remaining pastry and cut four 6 cm (2½ inch) rounds for pie lids. Place on a baking sheet lined with non-stick baking parchment and bake for 5-6 minutes until lightly coloured. Carefully lift the paper onto a wire rack.

8 For the filling, peel, core and cut each apple into 16 segments. Melt the butter in a wide shallow pan. Add the apple slices and fry gently until soft and transparent. (Add a little water to steam-cook the apples, if necessary depending on the variety.) Sprinkle on the sugar and allow to caramelise slightly.

9 For the crab apple sauce, pour the syrup from the jar of crab apples into a small pan and stir in the arrowroot. Heat, stirring, until slightly thickened and clear.

10 To serve, position the pastry cases on individual serving plates and fill with the apple slices, arranging them overlapping in circles. Top with the pastry lids. Surround with the crab apple sauce and place a poached crab apple on each plate. Place a scoop of ice cream to one side of each tart and decorate with a few toasted almonds. Dust with icing sugar and serve immediately.

Note: If you do not have any preserved crab apples, simply omit them; make a sauce by warming crab apple jelly and thinning it with a little water as necessary.

Lemon Tart with Fried Blackberries

Pastry:
175 g (6 oz) plain flour
125 g (4 oz) unsalted butter, in pieces
few drops of milk (if required)

Filling:
5 eggs
225 g (8 oz) caster sugar
finely grated zest of 2 lemons
juice of 5 lemons
200 ml (7 fl oz) double cream

Fried Berries:
25 g (1 oz) unsalted butter
25 g (1 oz) sugar
125-175 g (4 -6 oz) blackberries

1 To make the pastry, put the flour and butter into a food processor and work to a smooth dough; the mixture should form a ball without additional liquid, but if necessary add a few drops of milk.

2 Divide into 4 portions and use to line individual 10 cm (4 inch) flan tins. As the pastry is quite difficult to roll, you will find it easier to press the pastry directly into the tins, rather than roll it out first.

3 For the filling, whisk the eggs, sugar, lemon rind and juice together in a bowl.

4 Pour the filling into the flan cases and bake in a preheated oven at 180°C (350°F) mark 4 for about 40 minutes until set. Cool slightly in the tins before removing.

5 Meanwhile, melt the butter with the sugar in a frying pan. Add the blackberries and cook gently for 3-4 minutes.

6 Serve the lemon tarts on individual serving plates and surround with the berries. Serve with clotted cream.

Gingerbread Soufflé

175 g (6 oz) unsalted butter
175 g (6 oz) plain flour
250 ml (8 fl oz) milk
125 ml (4 fl oz) double cream
5 egg yolks (size 2)
225 g (8 oz) soft dark brown sugar
15 ml (1 tbsp) ground ginger
5 ml (1 tsp) ground cinnamon
2.5 ml (½ tsp) ground nutmeg
1.25 ml (¼ tsp) ground cloves
30 ml (2 tbsp) crystallised ginger, diced
7 egg whites (size 2)

To Decorate:
pieces of crystallised ginger

1 Butter 4 individual soufflé dishes, about 10 cm (4 inches) in diameter.

2 Melt the butter in a heavy-based saucepan. Whisk in the flour and cook, stirring, for 1 minute. Gradually stir in the milk and cream. Cook, stirring constantly, until thickened and smooth. Remove from the heat and let cool slightly for about 1 minute.

3 Add the egg yolks, one at a time, whisking well after each addition. Whisk in the brown sugar, breaking up any lumps, and continue whisking until the mixture is smooth. Stir in the ground ginger, cinnamon, nutmeg and cloves, then stir in the crystallised ginger.

4 Whisk the egg whites in a bowl until stiff but not dry. Fold into the soufflé base and pour into the individual soufflé dishes. Bake in a preheated oven at 200°C (400°F) mark 6 for 20-25 minutes until slightly puffed and lightly golden. Place each soufflé dish on a serving plate and scatter pieces of crystallised ginger on the plate to decorate. Serve immediately.

Italian Rice Creams with Cranberry Purée

600 ml (1 pint) milk
50 g (2 oz) caster sugar
1.25 ml (¼ tsp) freshly grated nutmeg
4 strips lemon zest
50 g (2 oz) Arborio rice
90 ml (3 fl oz) whipping cream
1 gelatine leaf
1 egg yolk (size 4 or 5)
15 g (½ oz) butter
1-2 drops of vanilla extract

Cranberry Purée:
225 g (8 oz) cranberries
40 g (1½ oz) caster sugar (approximately)

To Decorate:
mint leaves

1 Pour the milk into a saucepan. Add the sugar, nutmeg and lemon zest, stir well and bring to a simmer.

2 Add the rice and stir again. Turn the heat down to its lowest setting, cover and simmer for 40-50 minutes, stirring occasionally.

3 About 10 minutes before the end of the cooking time, pour the cream into a jug and add the gelatine leaf. Leave to soften.

4 When the rice is ready, add the egg yolk, butter and vanilla extract. Heat through, stirring, for 2 minutes. Take off the heat, add the cream mixture and stir until the gelatine is dissolved.

5 Pour the mixture into greased individual ring moulds or ramekin dishes and leave to cool completely. Cover with cling film and chill in the refrigerator for at least 1½ hours until set.

6 To make the cranberry purée, put the

cranberries and sugar in a saucepan and cook gently until soft. Taste and add a little more sugar if required. Transfer to a blender or food processor and work until smooth. Pass through a sieve into a bowl, cover and chill until required.

7 To serve, run a palette knife around the edge of each rice cream and turn out onto a serving plate; it may be necessary to give the mould a firm shake. Spoon the cranberry purée around the rice creams and decorate with mint leaves.

Black Cherry Clafoutis with Vanilla Ice Cream

Vanilla Ice Cream:
2 plump vanilla pods
250 ml (8 fl oz) milk
1 coffee bean, crushed
3 egg yolks (size 1)
70 g (2½ oz) caster sugar
125 ml (4 fl oz) double cream

Clafoutis:
2 eggs (size 1)
100 g (3½ oz) caster sugar
60 ml (4 tbsp) plain flour, sifted
pinch of salt
100 g (3½ oz) crème fraîche
100 ml (3½ fl oz) milk
15 ml (1 tbsp) kirsch
5 ml (1 tsp) vanilla extract
300 g (10 oz) bottled black cherries
  preserved in kirsch

Cherry Sauce:
375 ml (13 fl oz) red wine (preferably Syrah
  or Shiraz)
600 g (1 lb 5 oz) cherry compote
1-2 mint sprigs
icing sugar, to taste

1 To make the ice cream, split the vanilla pods open, scoop out the seeds and set aside. Pour the milk into a heavy-based saucepan, add the vanilla pods and coffee bean and bring slowly to the boil. Remove from the heat and set aside to infuse for 15 minutes. Meanwhile, beat the egg yolks, sugar and vanilla seeds together in a bowl until pale and creamy. Bring the milk back to the boil and pour through a sieve onto the egg mixture, stirring constantly. Return to the pan and cook over a low heat until the custard is thick enough to coat the back of a wooden spoon; about 3-5 minutes. Remove from the heat.

2 Stir the cream into the custard, allow to cool, then refrigerate for 1 hour. Transfer to an ice-cream maker and churn until thick. Turn into a freezerproof container and store in the freezer until required.

3 Butter a 22 cm (8½ inch) round ceramic baking dish for the clafoutis. Put the eggs in a bowl and whisk, using an electric beater until frothy. Add the sugar, flour, salt, crème fraîche, milk, kirsch and vanilla extract. Mix thoroughly for about 2 minutes. Allow to stand for 10 minutes.

4 Spread the cherries in a single layer on the bottom of the buttered dish. Pour over the batter and bake in a preheated oven at 200°C (400°F) mark 6 for 30-40 minutes until risen and golden.

5 Meanwhile, make the cherry sauce. Bring the wine to the boil in a small saucepan and reduce by half. Add the cherry compote and bring to the boil. Remove from the heat, add the mint and leave to infuse for 10 minutes. Add a little icing sugar to taste if necessary; the sauce should be slightly sour.

6 Serve the clafoutis with the cherry sauce and vanilla ice cream.

Warm Chocolate and Ginger Puddings with Caramelised Pears and Vanilla Custard

150 g (5 oz) quality plain chocolate
(Lindt Excellence or Valrhona)
15 g (½ oz) unsalted butter
3 eggs (size 2), separated
7.5 ml (1½ tsp) chopped preserved stem
ginger in syrup, drained
15 ml (1 tbsp) Calvados
45 ml (3 tbsp) caster sugar

Custard:
250 ml (8 fl oz) full-cream milk
1 vanilla pod
3 egg yolks
25 g (1 oz) caster sugar

Caramelised Pears:
1 firm, ripe pear
15 g (½ oz) clarified butter
15 ml (1 tbsp) brown sugar

1 Butter 4 ramekins and dredge with caster sugar to prevent the puddings from sticking.

2 Melt the chocolate with the butter in a heatproof bowl over a pan of hot water, then allow to cool. Stir the egg yolks, chopped ginger and Calvados into the cooled melted chocolate.

3 In a separate bowl, whisk the egg whites until they form soft peaks, then whisk in the sugar. Add a spoonful to the chocolate mixture to loosen it, then carefully fold the chocolate into the remaining whisked egg white mixture, retaining as much volume as possible.

4 Spoon the mixture into the ramekins, cover with cling film and refrigerate for at least 1½ hours.

5 Remove the cling film and place the ramekins on a baking tray. Bake in a preheated oven at 220°C (425°F) mark 7 for 15 minutes. Transfer the ramekins to a wire rack and leave to stand for 10 minutes.

6 In the meantime, make the vanilla custard. Pour the milk into a heavy-based pan, add the vanilla pod and bring to the boil. Lower the heat and simmer for about 5 minutes, then remove the pan from the heat and set aside for 5-10 minutes to infuse. Meanwhile, beat the egg yolks and sugar together in a bowl until pale and smooth. Pour on the hot milk, whisking constantly. Return the custard to the pan and cook over a low heat, stirring constantly with a wooden spoon until it is thick enough to coat the back of the spoon. Do not allow to boil or it will curdle. Quickly strain the custard through a fine sieve into a cold bowl, stirring to prevent further cooking.

7 For the caramelised pear, peel, halve and core the pear, then slice lengthwise. Heat the butter in a frying pan, then add the pear slices and sugar. Cook over a high heat, turning frequently, until caramelised.

8 To serve, turn the puddings out onto warmed serving plates. Serve with the caramelised pears and vanilla custard.

Note: If preferred the custard can be made in advance, quickly cooled by standing the bowl over a large bowl filled with ice, then refrigerated until needed. Cover the surface with a piece of dampened greaseproof paper to prevent a skin forming. Warm through gently to serve.

Warm Apricot and Almond Soufflés, with Apricot and Amaretto Ice Cream

Ice Cream:
450 g (1 lb) fresh or tinned apricots
100 g (4 oz) caster sugar
2 egg yolks
90 ml (3 fl oz) single cream
40 ml (1½ tbsp) Amaretto liqueur
90 ml (3 fl oz) double cream

Soufflés:
25 g (1 oz) ground almonds
finely grated zest and juice of 1 lime
75 g (3 oz) caster sugar
2 eggs (size 4 or 5), separated
90 ml (3 fl oz) double cream
25 g (1 oz) self-raising flour, sifted
1 fresh apricot, skinned, halved and stoned, or 2 canned halves, chopped
25 ml (1½ tbsp) flaked almonds

To Decorate:
15 ml (1 tbsp) flaked almonds, toasted and crushed
icing sugar, for dusting
blackcurrant sprigs
candied lime zest shreds (see note)

1 To make the ice cream, skin, halve and stone the fresh apricots if using. Roughly chop the apricots and place in a saucepan with 300 ml (½ pint) water and 25 g (1 oz) of the sugar. Bring to a simmer and cook gently until soft. Drain and press through a sieve into a bowl; let cool.

2 In a bowl, whisk the egg yolks with the remaining 75 g (3 oz) sugar until creamy. Put the single cream in a saucepan and slowly bring to the boil. Gradually pour onto the egg mixture, stirring. Let cool. Stir in the apricot purée and liqueur.

3 In another bowl, whip the double cream until it forms soft peaks, then fold into the apricot mixture until thoroughly incorporated. Transfer to an ice-cream maker and freeze according to the manufacturer's directions. (If you do not have an ice-cream maker, freeze in a shallow container, beating two or three times during freezing to break down the ice crystals and ensure an even-textured result.)

4 To prepare the soufflés, mix the ground almonds and grated lime zest together in a bowl. Beat in the sugar, egg yolks, cream and flour. Add the chopped apricot, flaked almonds and lime juice.

5 In another bowl, whisk the egg whites until soft peaks form. Stir half into the almond and apricot mixture to lighten it, then carefully fold in the rest.

6 Divide between 4 well buttered individual pudding basins. Stand in a roasting tin containing enough hot water to come two-thirds of the way up the sides of the basins. Bake in a preheated oven at 180°C (350°F) mark 4 for 50-55 minutes until risen and lightly browned on top. If the tops appear to be browning too quickly during baking, cover with discs of greaseproof paper.

7 Turn the puddings out onto individual serving plates, sprinkle with the crushed toasted almonds and dust with icing sugar. Decorate with the blackcurrants and candied lime zest. Serve with the ice cream.

Note: To prepare the candied lime zest, remove strips of lime zest from 1 lime, using a zester, and cut into shreds. Place in a saucepan with 150 ml (¼ pint) water and 25 g (1 oz) sugar. Heat gently until the sugar is dissolved, then simmer for 5-7 minutes. Remove with a slotted spoon and drain.

Half-baked Chocolate Mousse with a Coffee Grain Sauce

Chocolate Mousse:
200 g (7 oz) plain chocolate, in pieces
50 g (2 oz) unsalted butter
2 eggs (size 2)
15 ml (1 tbsp) caster sugar
15 ml (1 tbsp) plain flour

Coffee Grain Sauce:
3 egg yolks (size 2)
25 g (1 oz) sugar
300 ml (½ pint) milk
15 ml (1 tbsp) medium-grind coffee grains

To Serve:
175 ml (6 fl oz) double cream
icing sugar, for dusting
chocolate-coated coffee beans, to decorate

1 First make the coffee grain sauce. Lightly whisk the egg yolks and sugar together in a bowl. Meanwhile, pour the milk into a pan, add the coffee grains and slowly bring almost to the boil. Pour onto the egg mixture, whisking constantly, then strain into the top of a double boiler (or into a small heavy-based pan). Cook, stirring, over a low heat, until thickened enough to lightly coat the back of a wooden spoon; do not allow to boil or the sauce will curdle. Remove from the heat and leave to cool slightly.

2 Grease 4 individual loose-bottomed fluted flan dishes, about 7.5 cm (3 inches) in diameter, with unsalted butter.

3 Melt the chocolate with the butter in a heatproof bowl over a pan of simmering water. Let cool slightly.

4 Whisk the eggs and sugar together in a bowl, using an electric beater, for 5-10 minutes until doubled in volume, thick, creamy and almost white in colour. Sift the flour over the mixture and lightly fold in.

5 Fold the cooled melted chocolate into the mixture, then divide between the prepared tins.

6 Bake in a preheated oven at 200°C (400°F) mark 6 for 7 minutes until the edges have a cake-like texture, while the middle is still a little undercooked. The perfect result is a little cake-like chocolate mousse which is gooey inside! Leave in the tins for 10-15 minutes to cool slightly.

7 To serve, pour the coffee sauce around one side of each serving plate and pour the cream around the other side. Using a fork or a skewer, feather the sauces together, to create a pattern. Carefully remove each mousse from the tin and, using a palette knife, position on the sauce. Sprinkle with icing sugar and decorate with chocolate coffee beans. Serve at once, while the mousses are warm.

Note: Take care when removing the half-baked mousses from the flan tins as they are fragile.

Chilled Bread and Butter Pudding with Fruits, served with a Bramble Coulis and Crème Anglais

10 slices white bread (from 1 large medium
　　sliced loaf)
175 g (6 oz) butter
1 apple
grated zest and juice of ½ lemon
50 g (2 oz) sultanas
50 g (2 oz) dried apricots, chopped
300 ml (½ pint) double cream
300 ml (½ pint) milk
1 large vanilla pod
8 free-range egg yolks (size 2)
125 g (4 oz) caster sugar
freshly grated nutmeg
ground cinnamon, for sprinkling
30 ml (2 tbsp) thin honey

Bramble Coulis:
225 g (8 oz) blackberries
icing sugar, to taste

To Decorate:
mint leaves
few blackberries

1 Remove the crusts from the bread and lightly butter both sides. Line the base and sides of a 450 g (1 lb) loaf tin with buttered greaseproof paper. Line the base and sides of the tin with the buttered bread, cutting the slices to fit.

2 Peel, core and thinly slice the apple; place in a bowl of cold water acidulated with the lemon juice to prevent discolouration.

3 Mix the sultanas, chopped apricots and lemon zest together in a bowl.

4 To make the custard, put the cream and milk in a saucepan with the vanilla pod and slowly bring to the boil. Meanwhile, whisk the egg yolks and sugar together in a bowl. Gradually pour on the milk mixture, whisking all the time. Pour about three-quarters of the custard into a jug and flavour with a pinch of nutmeg. (Cover the rest of the custard and set aside.)

5 Sprinkle a thin even layer of the dried fruit mixture in the tin and cover with a single layer of apple slices. Lightly sprinkle with ground cinnamon. Cover with a layer of bread and butter, then pour on some of the nutmeg-flavoured custard. Repeat these until the tin is full, finishing with a layer of bread and butter. Pour on the rest of the nutmeg-flavoured custard.

6 Place the loaf tin in a roasting tin containing a 4 cm (1½ inch) depth of hot water. Bake in a preheated oven at 180°C (350°F) mark 4 for 30 minutes, then remove the foil and smear the honey on top of the pudding. Bake for a further 15 minutes or until a skewer inserted into the middle comes out clean.

7 Transfer the loaf tin to a tray of cold water to cool, then chill in the refrigerator.

8 Stand the bowl of reserved custard over a pan of hot water and stir until it is the consistency of double cream; allow to cool.

9 For the bramble coulis, press the blackberries through a nylon sieve into a bowl and sweeten with icing sugar to taste.

10 Cut the chilled bread and butter pudding into 1 cm (½ inch) thick slices and arrange on individual serving plates. Spoon the bramble coulis to one side and the vanilla custard around the other side of the plate. Decorate with blackberries and mint sprigs to serve.

Individual Summer Puddings with Crème Fraîche and a Raspberry Coulis

175 g (6 oz) caster sugar
350 ml (12 fl oz) water
1 vanilla pod
225 g (8 oz) raspberries
icing sugar, to taste
450 g (1 lb) mixed summer berries (eg
    strawberries, raspberries, blackberries,
    redcurrants), thawed if frozen
1 day-old thin sliced white loaf, crusts
    removed

To Decorate:
fresh berries
mint leaves

To Serve:
crème fraîche

1 Line four 150-175 ml (5-6 fl oz) individual pudding moulds with cling film, leaving a generous overhang. Place the sugar, water and vanilla pod in a saucepan. Heat slowly, stirring occasionally until the sugar has dissolved; set aside to infuse and cool slightly.

2 Crush the raspberries in a bowl, using a potato masher. Press through a fine nylon sieve into another bowl to remove the seeds. Add half of the puréed raspberries to the syrup with the berries. Heat gently for no longer than 5 minutes until the softest berries are just cooked. Remove from the heat.

3 Sweeten the rest of the raspberries with a little icing sugar to taste and set aside for the coulis.

4 Cut 4 rounds of bread to fit the base of the moulds, and 4 rounds to fit the tops. Shape the rest of the bread to fit the sides.

5 Remove the berries from the syrup with a slotted spoon and place in a bowl; set aside. Dip the shaped bread into the syrup to soak through, then use to line the base and sides of the moulds, reserving the 4 rounds for the tops.

6 Spoon the berries into the moulds so they are slightly overfilled. Position the tops and press down gently. Fold over the cling film to cover each pudding. Chill in the refrigerator for 1½-2 hours.

7 To serve, unmould each pudding on to a serving plate. Spoon the reserved raspberry coulis alongside. Decorate with fresh berries and mint. Serve with a generous spoonful of crème fraîche.

Chocolate and Orange Squares with a Dark Chocolate Coating and Piquant Orange Sauce

Chocolate Sponge:
80 g (3 oz) unsalted butter
65 g (2½ oz) caster sugar
1½ egg yolks
40 g (1½ oz) plain chocolate, melted
30 ml (2 tbsp) double cream
80 g (3 oz) self-raising flour, sifted
0.75 ml (⅛ tsp) baking powder
1½ egg whites

Chocolate Sauce:
25 ml (5 tsp) double cream
10 g (⅓ oz) unsalted butter
55 g (2 oz) dark plain chocolate, broken
* into small pieces*

Orange Sauce:
juice and grated zest of 2 oranges
juice of ⅓ lemon
55 g (2 oz) caster sugar
5 ml (1 tsp) cornflour, mixed with 15 ml
* (1 tbsp) cold water*
20 g (¾ oz) unsalted butter
20 ml (4 tsp) malt whisky

To Assemble:
40 ml (2½ tbsp) orange marmalade
few julienne strips of orange zest, to decorate

1 For the chocolate sponge, line a 12 cm (5 inch) square tin with non-stick baking parchment. Beat the butter and caster sugar together in a large bowl until light and fluffy. Add the egg yolks, melted chocolate, double cream, flour and baking powder and mix thoroughly. In a separate bowl, whisk the egg whites until they form soft peaks, then carefully fold into the cake mixture. Pour into the prepared tin and bake in a preheated oven at 180°C (350°F) mark 4 for about 20 minutes until cooked. Turn out onto a wire rack to cool.

2 For the chocolate sauce, put the cream and butter in a small saucepan and bring to the boil. Remove from the heat, immediately add the chocolate and stir until melted. Keep warm.

3 For the orange sauce, put the orange juice and zest, and the lemon juice into a saucepan. Add the sugar, stir until dissolved, then bring to the boil. Remove from the heat and stir in the blended cornflour. Return to the heat and cook, stirring constantly, until the sauce is thickened. Cook for a further 1 minute. Stir in the butter, then the whisky. Taste and add a little more sugar if necessary. Remove from the heat.

4 To assemble the dessert, trim the edges of the sponge, then cut into four 5 cm (2 inch) squares. Slice each square horizontally into three layers and sandwich together with the marmalade. Place each square in the centre of a serving plate. Pour on the chocolate sauce to coat the top of the sponge and drizzle slightly over the edges. Pour the orange sauce around the chocolate squares. Decorate with orange zest julienne and serve immediately.

Orange, Almond and Polenta Cake with Caramel Sauce

200 g (7 oz) unsalted butter
180 g (6 oz) caster sugar
200 g (7 oz) ground almonds
5 ml (1 tsp) vanilla extract
3 large eggs (size 1)
finely grated zest of 3 oranges
juice of ½ orange
100 g (3½ oz) polenta
3.75 ml (¾ tsp) baking powder

Caramel Sauce:
100 g (3½ oz) caster sugar
200 ml (7 fl oz) double cream

To Serve:
crème fraîche

1 Butter and flour a 20 cm (8 inch) loose-bottomed cake tin.

2 Cream the butter and sugar together in a bowl, using an electric mixer, until pale and fluffy. Stir in the ground almonds and vanilla, then beat in the eggs, one at a time. Add the orange zest and juice, polenta and baking powder; mix thoroughly.

3 Pour into the prepared cake tin and bake in a preheated oven at 160°C (325°F) mark 3 for 50 minutes to 1 hour, until set. Allow to cool slightly, then remove from the tin and transfer to a wire rack to cool.

4 To make the caramel sauce, melt the sugar in a small heavy-based pan over a gentle heat, then increase the heat and cook to a deep caramel. Remove from heat and whisk in the cream, taking care as the hot caramel will splutter. Reheat if necessary.

6 Serve the polenta cake warm or cool, with the caramel sauce and crème fraîche.

Blackcurrant and Honey Mousse wrapped in a Marzipan Pastry Parcel

For the marzipan pastry parcels, you will need to cut a cross template from a 1 mm thick plastic sheet (see below).

Mousse:
350 g (12 oz) blackcurrants
40 g (1½ oz) caster sugar
30 ml (2 tbsp) water
1 egg white (size 2)
2.5 ml (½ tsp) Gelozone (see note)
7.5 ml (1½ tsp) heather-scented honey
60 ml (2 fl oz) whipping cream, whipped

Marzipan Pastry:
200 g (7 oz) white marzipan
1 egg white (size 2)
5 ml (1 tsp) plain flour

Apple Sauce:
4 Granny Smith apples
90 ml (3 fl oz) water
50 g (2 oz) caster sugar
squeeze of lemon juice
½ vanilla pod, split lengthwise

Blackberry Sauce:
450 g (1 lb) blackberries
25 g (1 oz) sugar
7.5 ml (1½ tsp) crème de mûres liqueur

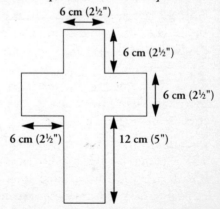

6 cm (2½")
6 cm (2½")
6 cm (2½")
6 cm (2½")
12 cm (5")

1 For the mousse, line a 12 cm (5 inch) square tin with greaseproof paper. Plunge the blackcurrants into a large pan of boiling water and blanch for 30 seconds. Drain well, then press through a fine nylon sieve into a measuring jug, to give about 225 g (8 oz) blackcurrant purée.

2 Put the sugar and water in a heavy-based pan and dissolve over a low heat. Bring to the boil and boil steadily until the syrup registers 120°C (248°F) on a sugar thermometer; ie the hard ball stage. Meanwhile, whisk the egg white in a bowl until it forms soft peaks, then whisk in the sugar syrup. Continue whisking at a medium speed until the meringue is cool. Add 50 g (2 oz) of the blackcurrant purée and continue beating until evenly incorporated.

3 Sprinkle the gelozone over the cold blackcurrant purée and stir until dissolved. Add the honey and heat for 1 minute to just below boiling point, stirring continuously. Leave to cool a little, then fold in the whipped cream, followed by the meringue mixture.

4 Pour the mousse into the prepared tin and place in the refrigerator for 4 hours or until set. Transfer to the freezer for at least 30 minutes.

5 To make the apple sauce, peel, core and chop the apples. Place in a heavy-based pan with the water, sugar, lemon juice and vanilla pod. Bring to a simmer and cook gently until the apples are tender. Let cool slightly, then discard the vanilla pod and purée the apples in a blender or food processor. Pass through a sieve and allow to cool.

6 To make the blackberry sauce, purée 125 g (4 oz) of the blackberries in a blender or food processor, then pass through a sieve into a saucepan. Add the

sugar and crème de mûres liqueur. Heat gently, then add the remaining blackberries. Cook gently for about 1 minute; do not allow to boil. Remove from the heat and allow to cool.

7 To make the marzipan pastry, put the marzipan in a food processor and work until finely ground. Add the egg white and flour and process to a smooth paste. Place the cross template on a baking sheet lined with non-stick baking parchment. Using a palette knife, spread a thin, even layer of the paste, about 1 mm thick, over the cut-out cross, then lift off the template. Bake in a preheated oven at 190°C (375°F) mark 5 for about 4 minutes, until golden brown.

8 Leave to cool on the baking sheet for about 1 minute, then carefully transfer the pastry cross to a second cool baking sheet, placing it upside down. Repeat to make at least 4 pastry crosses; a few extra will allow for breakages.

9 To assemble the parcels, carefully turn the mousse out of the tin. Trim the edges to neaten and cut into four 5.5 cm (2¼ inch) squares. Reheat a pastry cross in the oven for 3 minutes, or until pliable. Immediately after removing from the oven, place a square of mousse in the centre of the cross, quickly wrap up the pastry around the mousse to enclose, transfer to a cold plate and place in the refrigerator immediately. Repeat to make 4 parcels.

10 To serve, place each parcel on a cold serving plate and surround with the apple and blackberry sauces.

Note: Gelozone is a vegetarian alternative to powdered gelatine.

If the blackberries for the sauce have been frozen, simply coat them in the heated purée rather than cook them for 1 minute.

Japonais with Brandy Cream, Crushed Praline and an Espresso Sauce

Meringue:
4 egg whites (size 3)
150 g (5 oz) caster sugar
100 g (3½ oz) roasted almonds, finely ground
25 g (1 oz) cornflour
50 g (2 oz) icing sugar, sifted

Praline:
50 g (2 oz) sugar
50 g (2 oz) whole almonds, roasted

Brandy Cream:
*30 ml (2 tbsp) crab apple jelly (or other
   fairly sharp fruit jelly)*
50 g (2 oz) white marzipan, in small pieces
90 ml (3 fl oz) brandy
150 ml (¼ pint) whipping cream

Espresso Sauce:
30 ml (2 tbsp) unsalted butter
45 ml (3 tbsp) golden caster sugar
75 ml (5 tbsp) whipping cream
*45 ml (3 tbsp) freshly made strong espresso
   coffee*

1 For the meringue, whisk the egg whites in a large bowl until firm peaks form, then whisk in the caster sugar, a little at a time. When all the sugar has been added, the meringue should be glossy and stand in firm peaks. Gently fold in the ground almonds, cornflour and icing sugar.

2 Line two 30 x 20 cm (12 x 8 inch) Swiss roll tins with non-stick baking parchment and divide the meringue between the tins, spreading it gently and evenly. Bake in a preheated oven at 180°C (350°F) mark 4 for about 30 minutes until golden and just firm. Invert onto a wire rack, carefully peel off the lining paper and leave to cool.

3 Meanwhile, make the praline. Place the sugar and almonds in a heavy-based pan over a low heat until the sugar melts and turns a nut brown colour. Immediately remove from the heat and pour into a shallow oiled baking tin. Leave to cool until set hard, then break into pieces. Reserve a few shreds of caramel for decoration. Grind the rest of the praline in a food processor or blender; set aside.

4 To prepare the brandy cream, melt the jelly in a small pan. Take off the heat and beat in the marzipan, a piece at a time, until smooth. Beat in the brandy and leave to cool in the refrigerator. Whip the cream, then gently fold in the brandy mixture.

5 To make the espresso sauce, melt the butter in a small heavy-based pan. Add the sugar and stir over a low heat until dissolved. Add the cream, bring to the boil and boil steadily for 5 minutes. Add the coffee and boil again until the sauce is a light syrupy consistency. Take off the heat and allow to cool to room temperature. If the sauce thickens too much on cooling, stir in a little more coffee to thin.

6 When the meringue is completely cold, transfer to a board and cut out twelve 9 cm (3½ inch) rounds, using a sharp metal cutter. To assemble the japonais, for each serving sandwich 3 meringue rounds together with brandy cream, making sure the cream extends to the edge of the rounds. Smooth the sides and spread a little cream on the top.

7 To finish, cut 3 strips of greaseproof paper about 5 mm (¼ inch) wide and lay parallel on top of each tower. Sprinkle with crushed praline, then carefully lift off the strips of paper to leave a pattern. Place on large serving plates with a spoonful of espresso sauce. Decorate with shreds of caramel.

Lemon Genoese with a Lemon Cream Filling and Lemon Curd Sauce

Lemon Curd Sauce:
grated rind and juice of 1 lemon
25 g (1 oz) unsalted butter
50 g (2 oz) caster sugar
1 egg, beaten
20 ml (4 tsp) lemon liqueur

Genoese Sponge:
1½ eggs (size 3), beaten
35 g (1¼ oz) caster sugar
grated zest of 1 lemon
35 g (1¼ oz) plain flour, sifted
*10 g (⅓ oz) unsalted butter, melted and
  cooled until only just warm*

Lemon Cream Filling:
juice of ½ lemon
1 gelatine leaf
100 ml (3½ fl oz) crème fraîche
50 g (2 oz) caster sugar

To Decorate:
25 g (1 oz) plain dark chocolate
blanched lemon zest shreds

1 First make the lemon curd sauce. Put the lemon rind and juice, butter and caster sugar in a heatproof bowl over a pan of hot water until melted. Stir to mix thoroughly, then add the egg and stir with a wooden spoon until the mixture is thick enough to coat the back of the spoon. Remove from the heat and add the lemon liqueur. Set aside.

2 To make the sponge, whisk the eggs and sugar together in a large bowl over a pan of hot water, until the mixture is pale and thick enough to leave a ribbon trail when the beaters are lifted. Remove the bowl from the pan and continue whisking until the mixture is cool. Whisk in the grated lemon zest. Lightly fold in the flour. Pour in the butter around the edge of the bowl, and carefully fold in. Immediately pour into four lined ramekin dishes, 7.5 cm (3 inches) in diameter. Cook in a preheated oven at 190°C (375°F) mark 5 for approximately 5-8 minutes, until risen and just firm. Turn out onto a wire rack to cool.

3 For the lemon cream filling, warm the lemon juice, add the gelatine leaf and leave to soften. Mix the crème fraîche and sugar together in a bowl. Pass the gelatine and lemon juice mixture through a sieve into the bowl and mix thoroughly with the sweetened crème fraîche. Set aside to cool and thicken.

4 For the decoration, melt the chocolate in a heatproof bowl over a pan of hot water. Place the melted chocolate in a greaseproof paper piping bag and pipe a circle, about 6 cm (2½ inches) in diameter, on one side of each serving plate.

5 Using a 5 cm (2 inch) pastry cutter, cut out the centre of each sponge, then trim off ¾ cm (½ inch) from the base of these centres and discard. Dip the sponge centres into the lemon liqueur, then replace within the sponge rings.

6 Fill the sponge centres with lemon cream filling and decorate with lemon zest shreds. Carefully position a sponge on each plate next to the chocolate ring and fill the rings with the lemon curd sauce. Serve immediately.

Panna Cotta with Berries

Panna Cotta:
450 ml (¾ pint) double cream
2 vanilla pods, split
8 gelatine leaves, in smaller pieces
175 ml (6 fl oz) milk
50 g (2 oz) caster sugar

Hazelnut Biscuits:
50 g (2 oz) hazelnuts, chopped and toasted
50 g (2 oz) caster sugar
150 g (6 oz) plain flour
100 g (4 oz) butter, diced

Berries:
300 g (10 oz) raspberries
caster sugar, to taste
dash of crème de framboise liqueur, to taste
125 g (4 oz) each blackberries, redcurrants
and blueberries (or other summer berries)

1 For the panna cotta, put the cream in a saucepan with the vanilla pods and bring slowly to the boil. Remove from the heat and set aside to infuse. Meanwhile, soften the gelatine leaves in the milk for 10 minutes. Add the sugar, milk and gelatine to the warm cream and stir until dissolved. Set over a bowl of ice to cool. When the mixture begins to thicken slightly, pass through a muslin-lined sieve into a bowl, then divide between 4 individual moulds. Leave to set in the refrigerator.

2 To make the biscuits, finely grind the hazelnuts in a food processor. Add the sugar, flour and butter and process to a smooth dough. Wrap in cling film and rest in the refrigerator for 20 minutes.

3 Roll out the biscuit dough between 2 sheets of non-stick baking parchment until *very* thin. Trim to a large square and carefully lift (between the sheets of parchment) onto a baking sheet. Position a baking sheet on top and weight down to ensure a fine, crisp result. Bake in a preheated oven at 180°C (350°F) mark 4 for about 10 minutes. While still warm, cut out 4 rounds, using a cutter the same size or slightly smaller than the rim of the panna cotta moulds. Transfer to a wire rack to cool.

4 Purée 225 g (8 oz) of the raspberries in a food processor, adding sugar to taste. Pass through a nylon sieve into a bowl, then add the framboise to taste. Gently fold in all of the berries.

5 To serve, position a biscuit on each serving plate. Dip the panna cotta moulds briefly into hot water, then turn out onto the biscuit bases. Serve with the berries.

Citrus Crème with Fresh Orange Segments and a Grand Marnier Sauce

Caramel:
175 g (6 oz) caster sugar
100 ml (3½ fl oz) water

Citrus Crèmes:
200 ml (7 fl oz) double cream
90 ml (3 fl oz) milk
1 vanilla pod
3 eggs (size 2)
3 egg yolks (size 2)
125 g (4 oz) caster sugar
grated zest and juice of 2 lemons

Sauce:
15 ml (1 tbsp) liquid glucose
10 ml (2 tsp) sugar
grated zest of 1 orange
30 ml (2 tbsp) Grand Marnier
15 ml (1 tbsp) concentrated orange juice

To Serve:
1 orange, peeled and segmented
mint leaves
Tuiles (see right)

1 Butter 4 ramekins or other heatproof moulds with butter and sprinkle with caster sugar.

2 To make the caramel, put the sugar and half of the water into a heavy-based saucepan and heat slowly until the sugar is melted. Increase the heat and bring to the boil. Boil rapidly, brushing down the sides of the pan with a damp pastry brush to remove sugar crystals which might burn. Once the syrup reaches a dark caramel colour, immediately remove from the heat and carefully pour in the rest of the water, (protecting your hand as it will splutter). Pour a thin layer of caramel into each of 4 buttered individual ramekin moulds. (You won't need to use all of the caramel.)

3 To prepare the citrus crèmes, heat the cream, milk and vanilla pod together in a saucepan until just bubbling. Remove from the heat and leave to infuse. Meanwhile, whisk the eggs, extra egg yolks, sugar, lemon zest and juice together in a bowl until pale and smooth. Pour on the infused milk, whisking constantly until smooth. Strain through a muslin-lined sieve into a jug.

4 Divide the crème between the moulds. Stand them in a roasting tin containing enough water to come three quarters of the way up the sides of the moulds. Cover the moulds with foil and bake in a preheated oven at 170°C (325°F) mark 3 for 40 minutes until set. Remove the moulds from the roasting tin and allow to cool, then chill in the refrigerator for 1-2 hours, or until required.

5 Meanwhile, make the orange sauce. Melt the liquid glucose and sugar in a saucepan, add the orange zest, then the Grand Marnier. Flame the Grand Marnier then, when the flames die down, add the orange juice. Simmer to reduce to the required consistency.

6 To serve, unmould a crème onto the centre of each serving plate. Surround with the Grand Marnier sauce and decorate with fresh orange segments and mint leaves. Serve with the tuiles.

Tuiles

50 g (2 oz) icing sugar
15 g (½ oz) plain flour
40 g (1½ oz) butter
1 egg white (size 2)

To Finish:
icing sugar for dusting

1 To make the tuiles, mix all the ingredients together in a bowl until smooth, then leave to stand for 30 minutes.

2 Spoon the mixture into neat oval shapes on baking sheets lined with non-stick baking parchment, spreading it evenly.

3 Cook in a preheated oven at 150°C (300°F) mark 2 for 6-8 minutes until pale golden in colour. Whilst still warm and pliable, remove with a palette knife and place over a rolling pin. Leave to cool, then carefully remove and store the tuiles in an airtight tin to keep them crisp.

4 Dust with icing sugar to serve.

Pistachio and White Chocolate Frozen Mousse in Tuile Boxes on a Pink Grapefruit Sauce

To shape the tuile boxes you will need to make a cross template (see below), cut from a sheet of 1-2 mm (1/10 inch) thick plastic-coated card or stiffened foil. The template needs to hold the tuile mixture to form a cross. The cross which you cut out from the card or foil can be used to make the box moulds for the mousse. Simply fold and tape the sides together.

Pistachio Mousse:
1/4 gelatine leaf
60 ml (2 fl oz) milk
110 g (4 oz) white chocolate, in pieces
25 g (1 oz) skinned, ground pistachio nuts
1 egg (size 3)
1 egg yolk (size 3)
150 ml (1/4 pint) whipping cream

Tuile Biscuit Boxes:
50 g (2 oz) plain flour
50 g (2 oz) icing sugar
1 egg white
25 g (1 oz) butter, melted

Pink Grapefruit Sauce:
2 pink grapefruit
15-30 ml (1-2 tbsp) sugar
15-30 ml (1-2 tbsp) cocktail cherry syrup

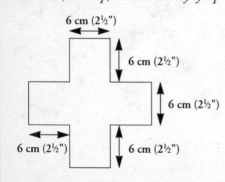

1 To make the mousse, soak the gelatine leaf in cold water to cover for about 10 minutes, until softened, then squeeze out excess water. Bring the milk to the boil in a saucepan. Remove from the heat and add the chocolate and gelatine leaf. Stir well until the chocolate is melted, then add the ground pistachios.

2 Whisk the egg and egg yolk together in a bowl until thick and creamy.

3 In a separate bowl, whip the cream until firm peaks form. Carefully fold the chocolate mixture into the cream, then lightly fold in the whisked eggs.

4 Divide the mousse between 4 box-shaped moulds, measuring 6 x 6 x 6 cm (2½ x 2½ x 2½ inches). Place in the freezer for 2 hours, or longer if possible.

5 To make the tuile boxes, sift the flour and icing sugar together into a bowl. Add the egg white and melted butter. Mix thoroughly until evenly blended.

6 Position the cross template (see left) on a baking sheet lined with non-stick baking parchment (or preferably bakoglide, if available). Spread a quarter of the tuile mixture very thinly over the cut-out cross area to cover evenly, then carefully lift off the template.

7 Bake in a preheated oven at 180°C (350°F) mark 4 for about 4 minutes or until just golden. Remove from the baking sheet as quickly as possible and carefully bend round a wooden cube to form the box shape. If it is too cool to mould, place the biscuit and box back in the oven for about 10 seconds to warm again. When firm, remove the wooden cube. Repeat with the rest of the mixture to make 4 boxes.

8 For the decoration, finely pare a few strips of grapefruit zest; set aside.

9 To make the sauce, peel the grapefruits, removing all skin and white pith, using a large sharp knife. Using a small vegetable knife, cut out the grapefruit segments, avoiding the membrane. Set aside. Squeeze the juice from the membrane into a small pan and add the sugar and cherry juice. Heat gently until the sugar is dissolved. Add the strips of grapefruit zest and simmer for 1 minute; remove with a slotted spoon and drain on kitchen paper. Add the grapefruit segments to the syrup and warm through. Carefully remove with a slotted spoon.

10 To serve, turn out each mousse onto an individual serving plate and cover with a tuile biscuit box. Arrange 3 grapefruit segments to one side of each mousse box. Pour the warm grapefruit sauce over the grapefruit and around the box. Decorate with the candied grapefruit zest.

Panna Cotta with Berry Compote

Panna Cotta:
375 ml (12 fl oz) double cream
400 ml (14 oz) can coconut milk
30 ml (2 tbsp) caster sugar
10 ml (2 tsp) rosewater
generous ½ sachet powdered gelatine

Berry Compote:
50 g (2 oz) caster sugar
60 ml (4 tbsp) water
juice of ½ lemon
*500 g (1¼ lb) mixed soft fruits (eg black-
    berries, raspberries, black and redcurrants)*

To Decorate:
mint leaves

1 Do not shake the can of coconut milk, but pour off about 125 ml (4 fl oz) of the clear liquid from the can into a cup and set aside.

2 Put the cream and coconut milk into a heavy-based saucepan. Bring slowly to boiling point, then reduce the heat and simmer, stirring occasionally, for 35 minutes.

3 Add the sugar and rosewater, stirring until the sugar has dissolved. Cook for a further 15 minutes.

4 Heat the reserved coconut liquid and sprinkle the powdered gelatine over the surface; stir until dissolved then pour into the cream mixture; stir thoroughly.

5 Divide the coconut mixture between 4 lightly buttered individual moulds. Stand the moulds in a deep baking tin containing iced water, to cool. Once cooled, transfer the moulds to the refrigerator and leave until set.

6 To make the compote, put the sugar, water and lemon juice in a heavy-based pan and heat gently until the sugar is dissolved. Increase the heat and boil for 1-2 minutes until syrupy. Add the soft fruit, bring back to the boil, then immediately take off the heat. Allow to cool.

7 To serve, briefly dip the panna cotta moulds into warm water, then turn out onto individual serving plates and surround with the berry compote. Decorate with mint leaves.

Mango and Passion Fruit Bavarois in Amaretti-covered Sponge, with Tropical Fruit Sauce

Sponge:

4 eggs (size 3)
100 g (3½ oz) caster sugar
40 g (1½ oz) butter, melted and cooled slightly
65 g (2½ oz) plain flour, sifted
2.5 ml (½ tsp) almond extract

Bavarois:

300 ml (½ pint) milk
4 egg yolks
100 g (3½ oz) caster sugar
20 ml (4 tsp) powdered gelatine
30 ml (2 tbsp) orange juice, or tropical fruit juice
1 large or 2 medium mangoes
5 passion fruit
300 ml (½ pint) double cream

Sauce:

100 ml (3½ fl oz) each pineapple, orange, mango and passion fruit juices, or 400 ml (14 fl oz) tropical fruit juice
30 ml (2 tbsp) sugar
10 ml (2 tsp) cornflour, blended with 15 ml (1 tbsp) cold water

To Finish:

30 ml (2 tbsp) apricot jam, warmed and sieved
8 amaretti biscuits, crushed
mint leaves, to decorate

1 To make the sponge, grease and line a 24 x 27 cm (9½ x 11 inch) Swiss roll tin with greaseproof paper. Whisk the eggs and sugar together in a bowl until thick and creamy, and the beaters leave a trail when lifted. Pour the melted butter around the edge of the bowl and carefully fold in, with the flour and almond extract.

2 Pour the mixture into the prepared tin and bake in a preheated oven at 190°C (375°F) mark 5 for about 15 minutes or until risen and firm to the touch. Turn out on to a wire rack, peel off the lining paper and leave to cool. Trim the edges of the sponge, then use to line the base and sides of a deep 900 g (2 lb) loaf tin.

3 To make the bavarois, slowly bring the milk almost to the boil in a saucepan. Meanwhile, whisk the egg yolks and sugar together in a bowl until pale and thick. Pour on the hot milk in a steady stream, stirring constantly. Return to the pan and cook over a low heat, stirring with a wooden spoon until the custard is thickened enough to coat the back of the spoon. Meanwhile, sprinkle the gelatine over the 30 ml (2 tbsp) fruit juice in a small cup and leave to soften for about 5 minutes. Stand the cup in a pan of hot water until the gelatine is dissolved, then pour it slowly through a sieve into the custard, stirring all the time. Set aside to cool.

4 Peel the mango(s) and cut the flesh away from the stone(s). Purée in a blender or food processor, then pass through a sieve into a bowl. Halve the passion fruit and scoop out the flesh and pips into a sieve. Press the passion fruit pulp through the sieve and mix with the mango.

5 In another bowl, lightly whip the cream until soft peaks form, then fold in the mango and passion fruit mixture. When the custard is on the point of setting, fold in the mango and passion fruit cream. Allow to cool slightly until thickened, then pour the mixture into the sponge-lined tin and place in the refrigerator for several hours until set.

6 To make the sauce, combine all the fruit juices in a pan, add the sugar and dissolve over a low heat, then increase the heat and reduce by one third. Stir in the cornflour and simmer, stirring, for 1 minute. Allow to cool and chill before serving.

7 To serve, turn the sponge out of the tin, brush with apricot jam and sprinkle over the crushed amaretti biscuits. Carefully cut into slices, using a sharp knife. Arrange 2 slices, slightly overlapping, on each serving plate and pour the tropical fruit sauce around. Decorate with mint leaves and serve at once.

Feuillantines with Caramelised Pears and Butterscotch Sauce

Feuillantines:
60 g (2 oz) plain flour
120 g (4 oz) icing sugar
2 egg whites
75 g (2½ oz) clarified butter, melted

Caramelised Pears and Nuts:
6 ripe pears (William or Conference)
40 g (1½ oz) caster sugar
40 g (1½ oz) unsalted butter
50 g (1¾ oz) shelled walnuts, roughly chopped

Butterscotch Sauce:
80 g (3 oz) sugar
pinch of salt
75 ml (5 tbsp) water
120 ml (4 fl oz) whipping cream
60 g (2 oz) unsalted butter

To Decorate:
mint leaves

1 To make the feuillantines, mix the flour, icing sugar and egg whites together in a bowl, then beat in the melted clarified butter. Spread the mixture very thinly onto 8 cm (3¼ inch) rounds on two baking sheets lined with non-stick baking parchment. (You will need 20 biscuits in total.) Cook in a preheated oven at 200°C (400°F) mark 6 for about 3 minutes until golden brown.

2 Carefully transfer the biscuits to a wire rack, using a metal spatula. Leave to cool. Store in a rigid airtight box until ready to serve.

3 Peel, core and chop the pears into small cubes. Place in a small pan with 15 ml (1 tbsp) of the sugar and cook over a gentle heat until just tender. Heat half of the butter and 15 ml (1 tbsp) sugar in a non-stick frying pan. Add the pear compote and cook over a high heat until caramelised. Remove and set aside. Heat the remaining butter and sugar in the pan, add the walnuts and caramelise over a high heat. Remove from the pan and leave to cool.

4 To make the butterscotch sauce, put the sugar in a heavy-based pan with the salt and 30 ml (2 tbsp) water. Place over a low heat until the sugar is dissolved, then increase the heat and cook to a golden brown caramel. Carefully add 45 ml (3 tbsp) hot water to thin down the caramel, then add the cream and bring to the boil. Stir in the butter. Pour the butterscotch sauce into a bowl and allow to cool.

5 To serve, pour the butterscotch sauce onto individual serving plates. Layer the biscuits in the centre of each plate, sandwiching them together with the pears and walnuts. Finish with a sprinkling of walnuts and decorate with mint leaves.

Almond Mousse Surprise with Raspberry and Mango Coulis

Biscuit Base:
75 g (3 oz) plain flour
50 g (2 oz) ground almonds
pinch of salt
75 g (3 oz) unsalted butter, softened, in pieces
1 egg yolk (size 2)
25 g (1 oz) caster sugar
1.25 ml (¼ tsp) almond essence
30 ml (2 tbsp) water

Almond Mousse:
7 g (¼ oz) (½ sachet) powdered gelatine
30 ml (2 tbsp) water
2 eggs (size 2)
40 g (1½ oz) caster sugar
30 ml (2 tbsp) Amaretto liqueur
50 g (2 oz) ground almonds
90 ml (3 fl oz) double cream

Raspberry Coulis:
225 g (8 oz) raspberries
50 g (2 oz) sugar
30 ml (2 tbsp) water

Mango Coulis:
2 medium, or 1 large mango(s)
50 g (2 oz) sugar
30 ml (2 tbsp) water

To Assemble:
7 g (¼ oz) plain chocolate
32 raspberries
12 blanched almonds
icing sugar, for dusting

1 First make the biscuit base. Sift the flour, ground almonds and salt together into a bowl. Rub in the butter until the mixture resembles crumbs. Add the egg yolk, sugar, almond essence and water and mix to a smooth dough. Wrap the dough in cling film and chill in the refrigerator for about 30 minutes.

2 Unwrap the pastry and shape roughly into a 15 cm (6 inch) round. Place on the middle of a baking sheet, lined with non-stick baking parchment. Cover the pastry with another sheet of paper and roll to a 3 mm (⅛ inch) thickness. Remove the top sheet of paper and prick the dough all over with a fork.

3 Bake in a preheated oven at 200°C (400°F) mark 6 for 8 minutes. Cut four 5 cm (2 inch) rounds, using a suitable cutter; remove the rest of the dough. Prick the rounds again and bake for a further 8 minutes. Remove from the oven and carefully transfer the biscuit rounds to a wire rack to cool.

4 Meanwhile, make the almond mousse. Sprinkle the gelatine over the 30 ml (2 tbsp) water in a cup. Leave to soften, then stand over a pan of simmering water until dissolved. Whisk the egg yolks with half of the sugar until pale, then add the Amaretto liqueur and dissolved gelatine, mixing well. Sift the almonds over the mixture and fold in lightly.

5 In a separate bowl, whisk the egg whites until firm peaks form, then whisk in the remaining sugar until stiff. In another bowl, whip the cream until thick, but not stiff. Fold the whipped cream into the almond mixture, then finally fold in the whisked egg whites.

6 Position four 6 cm (2½ inch) rings on a small board, on separate discs of greaseproof paper. Melt the chocolate in a bowl over a pan of hot water and paint the top of each biscuit with chocolate. Place a biscuit in the centre of each ring and fill around the edges with almond mousse, spooning just a little on top. Set 7 raspberries on each biscuit, away from sides, then cover with the mousse, smoothing the top. Place in the refrigerator for 3-4 hours or until set.

7 Meanwhile, prepare the coulis. Put the raspberries and sugar in a saucepan with the water. Heat slowly to dissolve the sugar, then bring to a simmer and crush the raspberries. Simmer to reduce by a quarter, then pass through a nylon sieve into a bowl to remove the pips.

8 Cut one 3 mm (⅛ inch) slice from the mango, cut 16 diamonds from this slice and set aside for decoration.

9 Peel the rest of the mango(s) and chop the flesh away from the stone(s). Put the mango flesh into a saucepan with the sugar and water. Heat slowly to dissolve the sugar, then bring to a simmer. Cook until the fruit is soft, then purée in a blender or food processor. Pass through a nylon sieve into a bowl. If the coulis appears too thick to spread easily, mix in a little water at this stage (see note).

10 To serve, dust one side of each blanched almond with icing sugar and caramelise under a preheated hot grill, let cool. Carefully lift each dessert ring with its paper and place towards one side of the serving plate, sliding the paper away as it is positioned. Run a warm knife around the inside of each ring to loosen the mousse, then carefully lift off the ring.

11 Decorate the top of each dessert with 3 almonds and a single raspberry, then dust with icing sugar. Surround the mousse with raspberry coulis and spoon the mango coulis into the other side of the plate. Feather the raspberry coulis into the mango coulis and place some mango diamonds in the raspberry coulis.

Note: The mango coulis should be slightly thicker than the raspberry coulis.

Floating Lemon Islands

For this dessert, you will need to prepare the sponge, lemon curd and vanilla custard in advance. Allow them to cool, then make the Italian meringue and construct the 'islands'.

Sponge:
2 eggs (size 2)
50 g (2 oz) caster sugar
50 g (2 oz) self-raising flour, sifted

Lemon Curd:
125 g (4 oz) caster sugar
finely grated rind and juice of 1 lemon
50 g (2 oz) unsalted butter, diced
1 egg, beaten (plus one extra yolk – optional)

Vanilla Custard:
1 vanilla pod, or 2.5 ml (½ tsp) vanilla essence
600 ml (1 pint) single cream
40 g (1½ oz) caster sugar
4 egg yolks (size 2)

Italian Meringue:
125 g (4 oz) caster sugar
75 ml (5 tbsp) water
2 egg whites (size 2)

Lemon Syrup:
30 ml (2 tbsp) caster sugar
30 ml (2 tbsp) water
15 ml (1 tbsp) lemon juice
30 ml (2 tbsp) dry sherry

To Decorate:
candied lemon peel
angelica pieces

1 To make the sponge, whisk the eggs and sugar together in a bowl over a pan of simmering water, until the mixture is very pale and creamy, and thick enough to leave a ribbon trail on the surface when you lift the whisk. Remove the bowl from the pan. Carefully fold in the flour.

2 Pour the sponge mixture into a greased and floured 25 x 15 cm (10 x 6 inch) Swiss roll tin and use a palette knife to spread the mixture out as evenly as possible. Bake in a preheated oven at 230°C (450°F) mark 8 for 5 minutes only; the sponge should be pale golden brown. Leave in the tin to cool.

3 To make the lemon curd, put the sugar, lemon rind and juice into a saucepan and heat gently until the sugar is dissolved. Add the butter and stir until just melted. Add the egg and cook over a *very* low heat, stirring constantly, until the mixture thickens; do not allow to boil. Pour into a bowl and allow to cool.

4 To make the custard, slit open the vanilla pod and scrape out the seeds; discard or reserve for flavouring another dish. Put the cream, sugar and vanilla pod into a saucepan and slowly bring almost to the boil. Remove from the heat and leave to infuse for 5 minutes, stirring occasionally. Meanwhile put the egg yolks into a large bowl and break them up with a fork. Bring the infused cream to the boil, then strain onto the eggs, stirring all the time. Pour the mixture back through the strainer into the saucepan.

5 Cook, stirring, over a very gentle heat until the custard thickens enough to lightly coat the back of the wooden spoon; do not allow to boil or it will curdle. Immediately take the pan off the heat and pour the custard into a clean bowl.

6 To make the meringue, put the sugar and water in a heavy-based saucepan and heat gently until dissolved. Increase the heat and boil the syrup steadily until it reaches the 'hard ball' stage, ie it registers 120°C (248°F) on a sugar thermometer (see note). Meanwhile, whisk the egg whites in a bowl until they form stiff peaks. Gradually pour on the syrup, whisking all the time. Continue to whisk for 3-5 minutes until the meringue is completely cool and very stiff.

7 To make the lemon syrup, put the sugar, water and lemon juice in a small pan and heat gently until the sugar is dissolved, then bring to the boil and boil until reduced to about 30 ml (2 tbsp). Remove from the heat and mix with the sherry.

8 Using a 7.5 cm (3 inch) plain circular cutter, cut 4 rounds from the sponge cake. Moisten the sponge rounds thoroughly with the lemon syrup. Spread each one generously with lemon curd. Pile the meringue on top of each one and neaten with a palette knife. Decorate with candied lemon peel and angelica.

9 Divide the custard between 4 soup plates. Decorate the edge of the custard with four blobs of lemon curd, running a toothpick through each to make a heart-shape. Now, using a palette knife, carefully lift an island to float on each dish of custard. Serve at once.

Note: To test the syrup for the 'hard-ball' stage, drop a little of it into a cup of cold water. It should immediately form a firm, pliable ball.

Chocolate Mousse with Raspberry and Cassis Sauce

Chocolate Mousse:
60 g (2 oz) plain chocolate, in pieces
40 g (1½ oz) white chocolate, in pieces
200 ml (7 fl oz) double cream
2 egg whites

Raspberry Sauce:
200 g (7 oz) raspberries
60 ml (4 tbsp) crème de cassis

To Serve:
fresh raspberries

1 To prepare the mousse, melt the plain and white chocolate separately in bowls over pans of hot water. Allow to cool slightly.

2 In another bowl, whip the cream until it forms soft peaks. Transfer two thirds of the whipped cream to another bowl and carefully fold the cooled melted plain chocolate into it. Fold the white chocolate into the smaller portion of cream.

3 In a clean bowl, whisk the egg whites until firm peaks form. Gently fold two thirds into the plain chocolate mixture, and one third into the white chocolate mixture. Lightly fold the two mixtures together to create a marbled effect.

4 Divide the mousse between 4 individual moulds and chill in the refrigerator until set.

5 To make the sauce, put the raspberries into a food processor and work to a purée, then pass through a nylon sieve into a bowl to remove the pips. Stir in the crème de cassis.

6 Turn out the mousses onto individual serving plates and add a generous swirl of the sauce. Decorate with fresh raspberries to serve.

Cointreau Ice Cream with Blueberry Coulis, served with Hazelnut Cookies

Home prepared fruit de bois is used for this recipe (see below), though crème de cassis can be substituted.

Ice Cream:
6 egg yolks
175 g (6 oz) caster sugar
60 ml (4 tbsp) Cointreau
finely grated zest of 2 oranges
600 ml (1 pint) double cream

Blueberry Coulis:
225 g (8 oz) blueberries
15 ml (1 tbsp) crème de fruits de bois (see below), or crème de cassis

Orange Zest Decoration:
knob of unsalted butter
5 ml (1 tsp) icing sugar
zest of 1½ oranges, shredded
splash of Cointreau

To Serve:
kumquat slices, to decorate
Hazelnut Cookies (see right)

1 To make the ice cream, beat the egg yolks and sugar together in a bowl until pale. Add the Cointreau and a quarter of the grated orange zest.

2 In another bowl, lightly whip the cream until thick enough to hold soft peaks. Lightly fold into the whisked egg mixture, with a metal spoon.

3 Transfer the mixture to an ice-cream maker and freeze according to the manufacturer's instructions. Alternatively spoon into a freezerproof container and freeze overnight in the freezer. (Due to the alcohol content this ice cream takes longer to freeze than other mixtures.)

4 For the blueberry coulis, purée the blueberries in a blender or food processor, then press the mixture through a fine sieve into a bowl. Add 15 ml (1 tbsp) crème de cassis or crème de fruits de bois.

5 For the decoration, melt the knob of unsalted butter in a small heavy-based pan with the icing sugar. Add the orange zest and Cointreau. Cook until caramelised, then pour onto a heatproof plate and leave to harden. Break into pieces.

6 To serve, scoop the ice cream onto individual plates and surround with the blueberry coulis. Position the caramelised orange zest on top of the ice cream and arrange a few kumquat slices to one side. Serve at once, with the hazelnut cookies.

Crème de fruits de bois: Soak 900 g (2 lb) mixed soft fruit, such as blackberries, raspberries and blackcurrants, in 1 litre (1¾ pints) red wine for 48 hours, then purée in batches, using a blender or food procesor. Pass through a jelly bag into a preserving pan, pressing the pulp to extract as much juice as possible. Measure the juice and add 900 g (2 lb) sugar to each 1 litre

(1¾ pints) liquid. Place the pan over a moderate heat and stir until the sugar has dissolved, then lower the heat and cook below simmering point for 1½-2 hours, until the liquid has reduced by about 5 mm (¼ inch) in depth and looks syrupy. Leave to cool overnight. The following day add approximately 900 ml (1¾ pints) brandy by pouring a tumblerful of brandy into a large bowl, then adding 3 tumblersful of syrup, continuing until all of the syrup is used. Pour into sterilised bottles and cork firmly.

Hazelnut Cookies

50 g (2 oz) hazelnuts, skinned
100 g (4 oz) plain flour
pinch of salt
75 g (3 oz) unsalted butter
50 g (2 oz) icing sugar
5 ml (1 tsp) vanilla essence
a little water to mix (if necessary)

1 Spread the hazelnuts out in a shallow baking tin and roast at 180°C (350°F) mark 4 for about 10 minutes until golden. Allow to cool, then finely grind in a food processor. Mix with the flour and salt.

2 Cream the butter and icing sugar together in a bowl, then add the vanilla essence. Stir in the flour and hazelnut mixture to form a smooth, stiff mixture. If it is too dry, mix in a little water.

3 Roll out the dough to a 5 mm (¼ inch) thickness and cut out shapes using a biscuit cutter. Carefully transfer to a baking sheet lined with non-stick baking parchment and cook in a preheated oven at 200°C (400°F) for 10-15 minutes until pale brown.

4 Leave on the baking sheet for a few minutes, then transfer to a wire rack to cool.

Yogurt Ice Cream with a Blackcurrant Coulis

Ice Cream:
500 g (1 lb 2 oz) Greek yogurt
80 g (3 oz) caster sugar
45-60 ml (3-4 tbsp) double cream
25 ml (1 fl oz) sugar syrup (see note)

Blackcurrant Coulis:
300 g (10 oz) blackcurrants
60 g (2½ oz) caster sugar (approximately)
few drops of lemon juice

To Decorate:
blackcurrants
redcurrants
mint leaves

1 Mix together the yogurt, sugar, cream and sugar syrup. Pass through a fine sieve into a bowl, then churn in an ice-cream maker until firm. Store in the freezer until required.

2 To prepare the coulis, put the blackcurrants, sugar and lemon juice in a blender or food processor and work to a purée. Taste and add more sugar if necessary. Pass through a fine sieve into a bowl, cover and chill in the refrigerator until needed.

3 To serve pour the blackcurrant coulis onto chilled serving plates. Place 3 scoops or quenelles of ice cream on each plate and decorate with blackcurrants, redcurrants and mint leaves. Serve at once.

Note: To make sugar syrup, dissolve 25 g (1 oz) sugar in 75 ml (5 tbsp) water in a heavy-based pan over a low heat. Bring to the boil and boil for 1-2 minutes. Allow to cool, then use as required.

Coconut Ice Cream in Brandy Snap Baskets

For this dessert, it is preferable to make the ice cream a day in advance and leave in the freezer overnight.

150 g (5 oz) coconut powder
300 ml (½ pint) whipping cream
300 ml (½ pint) Greek-style yogurt
15 ml (1 tbsp) sugar
30-45 ml (2-3 tbsp) Malibu

Brandy Snap Baskets:
125 g (4 oz) butter
125 g (4 oz) caster sugar
125 g (4 oz) golden syrup
125 g (4 oz) plain flour
5 ml (1 tsp) ground ginger

To Decorate:
mint sprigs
icing sugar, for dusting

1 Add the coconut powder to the cream, stirring to dissolve. Mix the coconut cream, yogurt, sugar and Malibu together in a bowl.

2 Pour into the ice-cream maker and churn for 20-40 minutes until thick and firm. Transfer to a freezerproof container, cover and freeze until required. (See note.)

3 To make the brandy snap baskets, put the butter, sugar and syrup in a saucepan and heat gently until dissolved and evenly blended. Remove from the heat and stir in the flour and ginger. Beat thoroughly and leave to cool.

4 Place 2 heaped teaspoonfuls of the mixture well apart on a greased baking tray and spread into rounds with the back of a spoon. Bake in a preheated oven at 180°C (350°F) mark 4 for 7-10 minutes until golden brown. Leave on the baking tray for about 1 minute to cool slightly, then carefully lift off with a palette knife and mould each one over a lemon or upturned ramekin to form a basket shape. When set, carefully remove the baskets and set aside. Repeat to make 5 or 6 baskets, to allow for any breakages.

5 To serve, set a brandy snap basket on each serving plate. Dip an ice-cream scoop into hot water, then scoop the ice cream into the brandy snap baskets, placing two scoops in each one. Decorate with sprigs of mint and dust with icing sugar. Serve immediately.

Note: If you do not have an ice-cream maker, freeze the ice cream in a shallow container, whisking the semi-frozen mixture several times during freezing to break down the ice crystals and ensure an even-textured result.

If the brandy snaps set firm before you have time to shape them, return the baking tray to the oven for ½-1 minute to soften.

Dark Chocolate Amaretto Ice Cream with White Chocolate Mousse

Ice Cream:
170 g (6 oz) caster sugar
60 ml (4 tbsp) water
100 g (3½ oz) plain chocolate, in pieces
45-60 ml (3-4 tbsp) Amaretto liqueur
600 ml (1 pint) whipping cream

Base:
16 amaretti biscuits
30 ml (2 tbsp) Amaretto liqueur

Mousse:
3 eggs (1 separated)
75 g (3 oz) caster sugar
5 ml (1 tsp) powdered gelatine
100 g (3½ oz) white chocolate, in pieces
140 ml (5 fl oz) double cream

To Decorate:
cocoa powder, for dusting

1 To make the ice cream, put the caster sugar and water in a saucepan and heat gently until the sugar is dissolved. Bring to the boil, lower the heat and cook for about 5 minutes until a syrup is formed, but not until it is caramelised. Leave to cool.

2 Meanwhile melt the chocolate in a heatproof bowl over a pan of simmering water, then slowly add the liqueur to taste. Leave to cool for 10 minutes.

3 Whip the cream in a bowl until soft peaks form, then whisk in the cool sugar syrup. Gradually fold in the melted chocolate.

4 Transfer the mixture to an ice-cream maker and churn until thick. (If you do not have an ice-cream maker, freeze in a suitable container; after 2-4 hours, when 2.5 cm (1 inch) ice cream has frozen around

the edges, return to the bowl and whisk for 10 minutes; return to the freezer; whisk twice more during freezing.) Once the ice cream is ready, store in the freezer.

5 For the base, crush the amaretti biscuits between 2 sheets of greaseproof paper using a rolling pin. Divide the amaretti crumbs between four 10 cm (4 inch) individual loose-bottomed tins, 2.5 cm (1 inch) in depth. Spread evenly and sprinkle with the liqueur. Press the crumb mixture well down and place the tins in the freezer.

6 To prepare the white chocolate mousse, place the 2 whole eggs, egg yolk and caster sugar in a bowl over a pan of simmering water and whisk until pale and creamy.

7 Meanwhile, sprinkle the gelatine over 15 ml (1 tbsp) water in a small bowl, allow to soften, then stand over a pan of simmering water until dissolved.

8 Melt the white chocolate in a heatproof bowl over a pan of simmering water, then leave to cool for about 10 minutes. Stir the cooled chocolate into the whisked egg, and then add the gelatine and mix thoroughly.

9 In another bowl, whisk the cream until starting to thicken. In a separate bowl, whisk the egg white until it forms soft peaks. Lightly fold the chocolate mixture into the cream until evenly incorporated, then slowly fold this into the whisked egg white.

10 To assemble, remove the tins from the freezer and half-fill with the ice cream. Carefully pour the white chocolate mousse on top until it reaches the top of the tins. Place in the freezer for 1½-2 hours.

11 Remove the desserts from the freezer 10 minutes before serving. Run a knife around the inside of the tins, and carefully transfer the desserts to individual plates. Dust with cocoa powder to serve.

Stag's Breath Ice Cream with Passion Fruit Coulis

Ice Cream:
125 g (4 oz) caster sugar
150 ml (¼ pint) water
4 egg yolks (size 3)
300 ml (½ pint) double cream
75 ml (5 tbsp) Stag's Breath liqueur
  (see note)

Passion Fruit Coulis:
6 passion fruit
15 ml (1 tbsp) concentrated orange juice
15 ml (1 tbsp) caster sugar
25 ml (1 fl oz) water

To Decorate:
raspberries
icing sugar, for dusting

To Serve:
Walnut Shortbread (see right)

1 To make the ice cream, put the sugar and water in a small heavy-based pan over a low heat until the sugar is dissolved. Bring to the boil and boil steadily for 2 minutes. Meanwhile, whisk the egg yolks lightly in a bowl. Gradually pour on the hot syrup, whisking all the time. Continue whisking for about 10 minutes until the mixture is light and doubled in volume. Allow to cool.

2 Meanwhile, whip the cream with the liqueur very lightly. Fold the cooled egg yolk mixture into the cream, then spoon the mixture into ramekins or small cups and place in the freezer until firm.

3 To prepare the coulis, halve the passion fruit and scoop out the seeds and pulp into a small pan. Add the orange juice, sugar and water and bring to the boil. Lower the heat and simmer gently for 2 minutes, let cool slightly, then transfer to a blender or food processor and process briefly. Pass through a sieve into a bowl and allow to cool.

4 To serve, scoop the ice cream onto the centre of each serving plate, and pour the passion fruit coulis to one side. Decorate with raspberries sprinkled with icing sugar. Serve with Walnut Shortbread Biscuits.

Note: Stag's Breath liqueur is a wonderful light liqueur made from fermented comb honey and fine whisky. If unobtainable, you could substitute Irish Mist.

Walnut Shortbread Biscuits

150 g (6 oz) plain flour
50 g (2 oz) caster sugar
50 g (2 oz) walnuts, very finely chopped
100 g (4 oz) butter, in pieces
caster sugar, for sprinkling

1 Sift the flour into a bowl and stir in the sugar and walnuts. Work in the butter, using your fingertips, until the mixture comes together. Knead lightly. (Alternatively, use a food processor. Process until evenly combined; do not overwork.) Wrap in cling film and chill in the refrigerator for about 1 hour to firm up.

2 Roll out the dough on a very lightly floured surface to about a 5 mm (¼ inch) thickness. Cut out biscuits, using a leaf-shaped cutter (or other cutter). Carefully transfer to a baking sheet lined with non-stick baking parchment.

3 Bake in a preheated oven at 170°C (325°F) mark 3 for 10-15 minutes (depending on size), until crisp and golden brown. Transfer to a wire rack and allow to cool. Sprinkle with caster sugar to serve.

Menus

Simon Jackson's Menu

Starter
Salad of Queen Scallops and
Crispy Smoked Bacon with
Walnut and Sesame Oil Dressing (p18)

Main Course
Fillet of Lamb with
Port and Mulberry Sauce (p81)
Baked Cabbage scented with Garlic
and Juniper (p94)
Julienne of Honey-glazed Carrots (p94)

Dessert
Individual Summer Puddings with
Crème Fraîche and a Raspberry Coulis (p128)

Colin Butter's Menu

Starter
Griddled Asparagus and Leeks
with Pecorino, on a bed of Socca (p36)

Main Course
Smoked Salmon and Cod Parcels, with Roast
Red Peppers, Tomato and Samphire (p52)
Individual Potatoes Dauphinois (p103)
Green Beans in Minted Vinaigrette (p88)

Dessert
Blackcurrant and Honey Mousse
wrapped in a Marzipan Pastry Parcel, served
with Apple and Blackberry Sauces (p130)

Chumki Banerjee's Menu

Starter
Warm Goat's Cheese Salad with Apple and
Celeriac (p38)

Main Course
Cod wrapped in Parma Ham, with Roasted
Peppers, Tomatoes and Aubergines (p51)

Dessert
Blackcurrant Tart with Lime Sorbet (p115)

Michael Boning's Menu

Starter
Fillet of Sole wrapped in Spinach with
Saffron Rice (p28)

Main Course
Breast of Gressingham Duck
Wildfowler-style (p60)
Potato Galettes (p106)
Creamed Purée of Leeks
Sautéed Carrots, Parsnips and Celeriac

Dessert
Individual Grape Tarts with Almond Crème
Pâtissiere and a Fruit Coulis (p111)

Carolyn Dyer's Menu

Starter
Quail Terrine with Morello Cherries
and Madeira (p30)

Main Course
Pot-roasted Venison in Fig Wine with
Mushrooms (p67)
Spicy Red Cabbage with Apple (p91)
Parmesan Puff Potatoes (p104)
Fine French Beans

Dessert
Dark Chocolate Amaretto Ice Cream with
White Chocolate Mousse (p147)

Andrew Whiteley's Menu

Starter
Salmon and Dill Paupiettes with a
Preserved Lemon Relish (p25)

Main Course
Bacon and Parsley Dumpling on a
Hot Apple, Walnut and Fennel Salad,
with a Tarragon-scented Tomato Sauce (p84)

Dessert
Chocolate and Orange Squares
with a Dark Chocolate Coating and
Piquant Orange Sauce (p129)

Mandy Ford's Menu

Starter
Chilled Thai Soup, served with Thai Salad and Prawn Won-Ton (p12-13)

Main Course
Poached Chicken "Hindle Wakes" with Lemon Sauce and Forcemeat Balls (p56)
Spinach and Cucumber Ribbons (p88)

Dessert
Quince Tart with Vulscombe Cheese Mousse and Figs in Rosewater Syrup (p 112)

James Hurd's Menu

Starter
Seared Scallop and Pancetta Salad with an Orange Saffron Dressing (p17)

Main Course
Pan-fried Duck on a Port and Wine Sauce (p65)
Potatoes Lyonnaise (p103)
Braised Cabbage Rolls (p92)
Root Vegetable Purée (p98)

Dessert
Pear and Almond Mille Feuille (p110)

Eveline Franklin's Menu

Starter
Warm Hot-smoked Wild Teifi Salmon on a bed of Pickled Samphire (p22)

Main Course
Boned Saddle of Welsh Lamb filled and topped with Crab Soufflé, served with a Red Wine and Tarragon Sauce (p76)
Baby Potato Kebabs (p106)
Julienne Leek Bundles (p88)
Medley of Steamed Beans

Dessert
Individual Apple Pies, served with Cardamom Ice Cream and Crabapple Sauce (p120)

Liz Franklin's Menu

Starter
Pan-fried Scottish Salmon on Wilted Greens with Spicy Tomato Sauce (p23)

Main Course
Fillet of Aberdeen Angus Beef roasted in a Salt Crust infused with Herbs (p70)
Caramelised Shallots and Garlic (p96)
Glazed Radishes (p98)
Horseradish Potatoes (p104)

Dessert
Citrus Crème with Fresh Orange Segments and Grand Marnier Sauce (p134)

Glen Tabor's Menu

Starter
Seafood Pastry Chests with Red Pepper Sauce (p20)

Main Course
Breast of Duck with Prune and Pistachio Stuffing, served with Prune and Madeira Wine Sauce (p61)
Potato and Wild Mushroom Cake (p102)
Tiered Shredded Vegetable Crowns (p95)

Dessert
Mango and Passion Fruit Bavarois in Amaretti-covered Sponge, with Tropical Fruit Sauce (p138)

Louise Halfhide's Menu

Starter
Double Tomato Tartlets (p40)

Main Course
Rosettes of Lamb with a Potato and Parsnip Rösti Crust, on a Wine and Redcurrant Sauce (p82)
Parsnip Crisps (p98)
Glazed Baby Carrots (p94)
Caramelised Shallots (p96)

Dessert
Warm Apricot and Almond Soufflés, with Apricot and Amaretto Ice Cream (p125)

Timothy Hobbs' Menu

Starter
Sautéed Scallops on a Cream Wine Sauce
flavoured with Saffron (p18)

Main Course
Roast Fillet of Scotch Beef on a Rich
Red Wine Sauce (p72)
Potato and Parsnip Rösti (p100)
Roast Shallots and Garlic
Steamed Mangetout
Buttered Baby Carrots with Fresh Herbs

Dessert
Chilled Bread and Butter Pudding with Fruits,
a Bramble Coulis and Crème Anglais (p127)

Wendy Burnley's Menu

Starter
Smoked Bacon and Queenie Salad with a
Warm Vinaigrette Dressing (p15)

Main Course
Fillet of Lamb with a Madeira Sauce (p75)
Potatoes Dauphinois (p103)
Roast Parsnip 'Cups' with Parsnip Purée (p99)
Savoury Spinach with Lamb's Kidney (p90)

Dessert
Lemon and Almond Tart, with a Lemon
Sabayon Sauce and Amaretto Cream (p116)

Juliette Boisseau-Hardman's Menu

Starter
Salad of Cooked Peppers with a
Saffron Vinaigrette (p39)

Main Course
Grilled Sea Bass with Fennel Butter
and Cucumber Noodles (p45)
Sautéed Potatoes (p102)

Dessert
Feuillantines with Caramelised Pears
and Butterscotch Sauce (p139)

Tommy Sheppard's Menu

Starter
King Prawns with Pear (p15)

Main Course
Fillet of Lamb on a Root Vegetable Plinth,
with a Port and Lemon Gravy (p78)
Stuffed Savoy Cabbage (p92)
Raspberried Red Cabbage (p91)

Dessert
Grapefruit Tart with Orange Sauce
and Vanilla Cream (p118)

Amanda Farnese's Menu

Starter
Oxtail Soup with Herb Dumplings (p11)

Main Course
Cod and Coriander on a bed of Leeks
with Parmesan (p51)
Saffron Mash (p105)

Dessert
Lemon Tart with Fried Berries
and Clotted Cream (p121)

Barbara Vazana's Menu

Starter
Arbroath Smokie and Mussel Chowder (p10)

Main Course
Angus Steak with Whisky and
Green Peppercorn Sauce (p71)
Mejadarra with Mushrooms (p107)
Beetroot and Preserved Lime Salad (p97)

Dessert
Panna Cotta with Berry Compote (p137)

Michael Collins' Menu

Starter
Salmon and Matzomeal Fishcakes with
an Orange Pepper Sauce (p24)

Main Course
Pan-fried Breast of Wild Cotswold Mallard
with a Port Sauce, Wild Mushrooms and
Caramelised Shallots (p62)
Spinach Purée with Pine Nuts (p90)
Creamed Potatoes with Truffle (p105)

Dessert
Almond Mousse Surprise, served with
Raspberry and Mango Coulis (p140)

Marian Freeman's Menu

Starter
Devilled Chicken Livers with Walnuts
on a Mixed Leaf Salad (p31)

Main Course
Steamed Fillet of Red Snapper with Courgettes
and Shallots on a Watercress Sauce (p48)
Cheese and Sesame Tuile filled with
Baby Vegetables (p95)
Fried Potato Shavings

Dessert
Japonais with Brandy Cream, Crushed Praline
and an Espresso Sauce (p132)

Neil Haidar's Menu

Starter
Leek and Goat's Cheese Ravioli
with Gremolata (p33)

Main Course
Pan-fried John Dory with Wild Mushrooms
and Chinese 'Seaweed' (p54)

Dessert
Warm Chocolate and Ginger Pudding,
with Caramelised Pears and
Vanilla Custard (p124)

Judith Elliott's Menu

Starter
Monkfish with Lemon and Caperberry
Vinaigrette (p29)

Main Course
Roast Rack of Lamb with a Rosemary and
Port Sauce (p79)
Anna Potatoes (p105)
Carrots with Cumin (p94)

Dessert
Italian Rice Creams with
Cranberry Purée (p122)

Claire Ketteman's Menu

Starter
Beetroot Mousse with Horseradish Sauce (p35)

Main Course
Salmon Parcels with Lime and Coriander
Beurre Blanc (p53)
Potato and Courgette Soufflés (p101)

Dessert
Damson Tart with Meringue Topping (p117)

Alison Kay's Menu

Starter
Double-baked Onion Soufflé with a
Truffle Oil Dressing (p34)

Main Course
Medallions of Ostrich stuffed with Scallops,
served with a Tortellini of Tunip Tops and a
Cardamom and Vanilla Sauce (p64)

Dessert
Pistachio and White Chocolate
Frozen Mousse in Tuile Boxes on a
Pink Grapefruit Sauce (p136)

Charlotte Bircher's Menu

Starter
Tarte à l'Oignon (p36)

Main Course
*Pork wrapped in Spinach and Bacon
with a Mushroom Stuffing (p85)
Parsnip Purée with Parmesan (p99)
Broccoli
Spinach*

Dessert
*Cointreau Ice Cream with Blueberry Coulis,
served with Hazelnut Cookies (p144-5)*

Andrew Urbanek's Menu

Starter
*Mixed Herb Salad with Quail's Eggs,
Pancetta and Parmesan (p37)*

Main Course
*Poached Turbot on Creamed Spinach and Fresh
Tagliatelle, served with a Tomato Butter Sauce
and Roast Cherry Tomatoes (p46)*

Dessert
*Pear and Almond Tart with
Amaretto Ice Cream (p114)*

Noriko Anzai-Jackson's Menu

Starter
Seafood Dumplings (p21)

Main Course
*Chicken Sauté in Ginger Sauce with
Japanese Mushroom Fritters (p58)
Parsley Rice (p108)
Three-colour Vegetable Stir-fry (p90)*

Dessert
*Chocolate Mousse with Raspberry and
Cassis Sauce (p143)*

Semi-final Menu

Starter
Nage of Scallops with a Vegetable Julienne (p17)

Main Course
*Saddle of Roe Deer with a Port Sauce (p68)
Buttered Spinach with Nutmeg (p90)
Parsley Potatoes (p101)*

Dessert
*Yogurt Ice Cream with a
Blackcurrant Coulis (p145)*

Semi-final Menu

Starter
*Seared Scallops with Spring Greens and
Red Pepper Sauce (p19)*

Main Course
*Grilled Fillet of Lamb with
Spiced Couscous (p80)*

Dessert
*Orange, Almond and Polenta Cake,
with Caramel Sauce (p130)*

Semi-final Menu

Starter
*Mussels with Blue Vinney Sauce, served with
Walnut Bread (p16)*

Main Course
*"Hong Kong" Steak Pie with Marinated
Pigeon Breast (p73)
Salud's Cabbage (p93)
Steamed Mangetout*

Dessert
Floating Lemon Islands (p142)

Semi-final Menu

Starter
Lobster and Isle of Skye Scampi Risotto (p22)

Main Course
Fillet of Aberdeen Angus Beef with Buttered
Spinach and Parsnip Chips (p74)
Horseradish Bubble and Squeak (p100)

Dessert
Treacle Tart with Lemon Zest and
Custard Sauce (p113)

Semi-final Menu

Starter
Grilled Haddock Fillet with a Cheese and Dill
Topping, served with a Cranberry and Red
Pepper Marmalade (p26)

Main Course
Stuffed Pigeon Breast wrapped in
a Lattice Puff Pastry Crust, served with
an Elderberry Sauce (p66)
Puréed Parsnip Timbales (p99)
Lemon-glazed Carrot Ribbons (p94)

Dessert
Lemon Genoese with a Lemon Cream Filling
and Lemon Curd Sauce (p133)

Semi-final Menu

Starter
Polenta with Home-dried Tomatoes,
Mozzarella, Basil and an Olive Tapenade (p41)

Main Course
Guinea Fowl Breasts with Calvados,
Apple and Onion Sauce (p 59)
Broccoli Timbales (p89)
Butternut Squash Balls (p98)

Dessert
Gingerbread Soufflé (p122)

Semi-final Menu

Starter
Crab Salad with Chilli and
Herb Dressing (p14)

Main Course
Brill with Mushroom Hollandaise
and Herb Sauce (p49)
Stoved Potatoes (p105)
Glazed Green Beans (p88)

Dessert
Raspberry Tart with Vanilla Ice Cream (p119)

Semi-final Menu

Starter
Roasted Red Pepper and Tomato Soup (p12)

Main Course
Fillet of Pork with Prunes (p86)
Creamed Polenta (p108)
Broccoli with Crisp Pancetta (p89)

Dessert
Coconut Ice Cream in
Brandy Snap Baskets (p146)

Semi-final Menu

Starter
Black Pudding en Croûte with Mulberry-dressed
Salad Leaves (p42)

Main Course
Roast Sea Bass with Braised Fennel and
a Bloody Mary Sauce (p44)
Aubergine Crisps (p97)

Dessert
Stag's Breath Ice Cream with
Passion Fruit Coulis, served with
Walnut Shortbread (p148)

Final Menu

Starter
*Pan-fried Red Mullet with
Braised Fennel (p 27)*

Main Course
*Roasted Chicken with Wild Mushrooms
Potato and Celeriac Mash (p 57)*

Dessert
*Black Cherry Clafoutis with
Vanilla Ice Cream (p 123)*

Final Menu

Starter
*Lemon Risotto with Fresh Herb Salad,
served with Parmesan Tuiles (p 32)*

Main Course
*Turbot with Leeks and Wild
Mushrooms (p 47)
Crispy Potatoes (p 102)*

Dessert
Panna Cotta with Fresh Berries (p 134)

Final Menu

Starter
*Pesto Fish Cakes with a
Roasted Red Pepper Salsa (p 26)*

Main Course
*Pan-fried Fillet of Lamb with Rosemary, Roasted
Aubergine and Garlic, Caramelised Plum
Tomatoes and Couscous (p 83)*

Dessert
*Half-baked Chocolate Mousse with a
Coffee Grain Sauce (p 126)*

1996 MasterChef Judges

Germain Schwab • Ulrika Jonnson • Sean Davies • Derek Johns
Imogen Stubbs • Jonathan Wicks • Jenni Murray • Darina Allen • Nigel Havers
Gary Rhodes • Geraldine James • Gordon Ramsey • Allan Lamb • David Adlard
Jancis Robinson • Bruce Sangster • Norman Painting • Maddalena Bonino
Andrew Neil • Eugine McCoy • Nicole Farhi • Rose Gray • Michael Chow
Herbert Berger • Richard Wilson • Michel Roux • Sir Richard Rogers

Index